W9-AZT-740

Studying God's Word
Book A

Seymour Loveland

Christian Liberty Press
Arlington Heights, Illinois

ORIGINAL TITLES: *The Illustrated Bible Story Book, Old Testament,* © 1923
and *The Illustrated Bible Story Book, New Testament,* © 1925
ORIGINAL PUBLISHER: Rand McNally & Company, Chicago
ILLUSTRATOR: Milo Winter, for both *Old* and *New Testaments* stories

This book is a compilation of Bible stories retold by Seymour Loveland.

Copyright © 1996 by Christian Liberty Press
2007 Printing

All Rights Reserved. No part of this book may be reproduced or transmitted in any form or by any means, electronic or mechanical, without written permission from the publisher. Brief quotations embodied in critical articles or reviews are permitted.

A publication of

Christian Liberty Press

502 West Euclid Avenue
Arlington Heights, Illinois 60004
www.christianlibertypress.com

ISBN 978-1-930092-56-3
1-930092-56-3

Printed in the United States of America

Contents

Preface

One of the primary goals of the *Studying God's Word* series is to encourage students to conform their thinking to the standard of God's revealed Word. When students begin to bring every thought into captivity to Scripture, they begin to realize the joy of being conformed to the image of Jesus Christ.

This book is a compilation of stories from Seymour Loveland's *The Illustrated Bible Story Books, Old Testament* (Rand McNally © 1923) and *New Testament* (Rand McNally © 1925). Loveland closely follows the Bible narrative, adding nothing except what seemed necessary to give fuller understanding to the young mind. Comprehension exercises have also been provided throughout the book to help students recall the biblical content that is presented.

In the hope that this book may be useful in promoting a love for God's Word among old and young alike, it is sent forth on its mission.

—The Publishers

What a Good Child Loves

I love the Lord who died for me,

I love His little child to be;

I love the Bible, where I find

How good my Savior was, and kind;

I love His people and their ways,

I love with them to pray and praise;

I love the Father and the Son,

And Holy Spirit, three in one;

I love to think the time will come

When I shall be in heaven my home.

Stories From The Old Testament

1 The First Baby in the World and His Brother

GENESIS 3:1–4:17

The first man's name was Adam and his wife was called Eve. They lived in a beautiful garden away in the east country which was called Eden. The garden was filled with beautiful trees and flowers of all kinds. But they did not live in Eden long for they did not obey God's command. They ate the fruit of a tree which had been forbidden them. They were driven forth by an angel and had to give up their beautiful garden home.

So Adam and his wife went out into the world to live and to work. For a time they were all alone, but after a while God gave them a little child of their own, the first baby that ever came into the world. They named him Cain. A few years later, another baby came whom they named Abel.

When the two boys grew up, they worked, as their father worked before them. Cain, the older brother, chose to work in the fields, and raised grain and fruits. Abel, the younger brother, had a flock of sheep and became a shepherd.

While Adam and Eve were living in the Garden of Eden, they could talk with God and hear God's voice speaking to them. But now that they were out in the world, they could no longer talk with God freely, as before. The sin of Adam had broken the friendship between God and mankind. So when they came to God, they built an altar of stones and laid upon it, something as a gift to God, and burned it, to show that it

Adam and Eve Driven from the Garden of Eden

Cain's Jealousy over Abel's Sacrifice

was given to God, whom they could not see. Then before the altar, they prayed to God, and asked God to forgive their sins. They also prayed to God to bless them and do good to them.

Each of these brothers, Cain and Abel, offered upon the altar to God his own gift. Cain brought the fruits and the grain which he had grown. Abel brought a sheep from his flock, and killed it and burned it upon the altar.

God was pleased with Abel and his offering, but was not pleased with Cain's offering. God wished Cain to offer a blood sacrifice, as Abel offered. Cain's heart was not right when he came before God to worship because he tried to approach God on his own terms.

God showed that He was not pleased with Cain. Cain, instead of being sorry for his sin, and asking God to forgive him, was very angry with God, and angry also toward his brother Abel. When they were out in the field together, Cain struck his brother Abel and killed him. So the first baby in the world grew up to be the murderer of his own brother.

And the Lord said to Cain, "Where is Abel, your brother?"

And Cain answered, "I do not know; why should I take care of my brother?"

Then the Lord said to Cain "What is this that you have done? Your brother's blood is like a voice crying to me from the ground. Do you see how the ground has opened, like a mouth, to drink your brother's blood? As long as you live, you shall be under God's curse for the murder of your brother. You shall wander over the earth, and shall never find a home, because you have done this wicked deed."

And Cain said to the Lord, "My punishment is greater than I can bear. Thou hast driven me out from among men; and thou hast hid thy grace from me. If any man finds me he will kill me, because I shall be alone, and no one will be my friend."

And God said to Cain, "If anyone harms Cain, he shall be punished for it." And the Lord God placed a mark on Cain, so that whoever met him should know him, and should know also that God had forbidden any man to harm him. Then Cain and his wife went away from Adam's home to live in a place by themselves, and there they had children. And Cain's family built a city in that land; and Cain named the city after his first child, whom he had called Enoch.

Comprehension Exercise

Complete the sentences using the words below.

Abel
Adam
Eden
Cain

1. The first man was named

   _____.

2. The name of the first baby that was born in the world was

   _____.

3. _____ was murdered by his brother.

4. Adam and Eve lived first in the garden of

   _____.

2 The Big Ship That God Used to Save Eight People

GENESIS 5:1—9:17

After Abel was slain, and his brother Cain had gone into another land, God gave another child to Adam and Eve. This child they named Seth; and other sons and daughters were given to them; for Adam and Eve lived many years. But at last they died, as God had said that they must die, because they had eaten of the tree that God had forbidden them to eat.

By the time that Adam died, there were many people on the earth. Over the years, the children of Adam and Eve had many other children; and when these grew up they had other children; and these had children also. People in those early times lived much longer than they do now. Very few people now live to be a hundred years old; but in those days, when the earth was new, men often lived to be around eight hundred years old. So after a time that part of the earth where Adam's sons lived began to be full of people.

It is sad to tell that as time went on more and more of these people became wicked, and fewer and fewer of them grew up to become good men and women. All the people lived close together. Only a few went away to other lands. For this reason, even the children of good men and women learned to be bad, like the people around them.

And as God looked down on the world that He had made, He saw how wicked the men in it had become, and that every thought and every act of man was continually evil.

But while most of the people in the world were very wicked, there were some good people also, though they were very few. The best of all the men who lived at that time was a man whose name was Enoch. He was not the son of Cain, but another Enoch, who came from the family of Seth, the son of Adam, who was born after the death of Abel. While so many around Enoch were doing evil, this man did only what was right. He walked with God and God walked with him, and talked with him. And at last, when Enoch was three hundred and sixty-five years old, God took him away from earth to heaven. He did not die, as all the people have since Adam disobeyed God, but "he was not, for God took him." This means that Enoch was taken up from earth without dying.

Enoch left a son whose name was Methuselah. We do not know anything about Methuselah, except that he lived to be nine hundred and sixty-nine years old, which was longer than the life of any other man who ever lived. But at last Methuselah died like all his people, except his father Enoch. By the time that Methuselah died, the world was very wicked. And God looked down on the earth and said:

"I will take away all men from the earth that I have made; because the men of the world are evil, and evil continually."

But even in those bad times God saw one good man. His name was Noah. Noah tried to do right in the sight of God. As Enoch had walked with God, so Noah walked with God, and talked with him. And Noah had three sons; their names were Shem, Ham, and Japheth.

God said to Noah, "The time has come when all the men and women on the earth are to be destroyed. Everyone must die, because they are all wicked. But you and your family shall be saved, because you alone are trying to do right."

Then God told Noah how he might save his life and the lives of his sons. He was to build a very large boat, as large as the largest ships that are made in our time. It was to be very long, and very wide and very deep; with a roof over it. Such a ship as this was called an "ark." God told Noah to build this ark, and to have it ready for the time when he would need it.

"For," said God to Noah, "I am going to bring a great flood of water on the earth, to cover all the land, and to drown all the people on the earth. And as the animals on the earth will be drowned with the people, you must make the ark large enough to hold a pair of each kind of animal, and several pairs of some animals that are needed by men, like sheep and goats and oxen; so that there will be animals as well as men to live upon the earth after the flood has passed away. And you must take in the ark food for yourself and your family, and for all the animals with you; enough food to last for a year, while the flood shall stay on the earth."

And Noah did what God told him to do, although it must have seemed very strange to all the people around, to build this great ark where there was no water for it to sail upon. And it was a long time, even a hundred and twenty years, that Noah and his sons were at work building the ark. The wicked people who lived nearby often wondered, and no doubt laughed at Noah for building a large ship where there was no sea.

At last the ark was finished, and stood like a great house on the land. There was a door on one side, and a window on the roof, to let in the light. Then God said to Noah:

"Come into the ark, you and your wife, and your three sons, and their wives with them; for the flood of waters will come very soon. And take with you animals of all kinds, and birds, and things that creep; seven pairs of those that will be needed by men, and one pair of all the rest, so that all kinds of animals may be kept alive upon the earth."

So Noah and his wife, and his three sons, Shem, Ham and Japheth, with their wives, went into the ark. And God brought to the door of the ark the animals, and the birds, and the creeping things of all kinds; and they went into the ark. And Noah and his sons put them in their places, and brought in food enough to feed them

all for many days. And then the door of the ark was shut so that no more people and no more animals could come in.

In a few days the rain began to fall, as it had never rained before. It seemed as though the heavens were opened to pour great floods upon the earth. The streams filled, and the rivers rose higher and higher, and the ark began to float on the water. The people left their houses and ran up to the hills; but soon the hills were covered, and all the people on them were drowned.

Some had climbed up to the tops of higher mountains, but the water rose higher and higher, until even the mountains were covered. All the wicked people were drowned. At this same time, all the wild animals, lions, and tigers, and all the rest were also drowned. Even the birds were drowned, for their nests in the trees were swept away, and there was no place where they could fly from the terrible storm. For forty days and nights the rain kept on, until there was no breath of life remaining outside of the ark.

After forty days the rain stopped, but the water stayed upon the earth for more than six months. The ark with all that were in it floated over the great sea that covered the land.

Then God sent a wind to blow over the waters, and to dry them up. Little by little, the waters grew less and less. First the mountains rose above the waters, then the hills rose up. Finally the ark ceased to float and lay aground on a mountain which is called Mount Ararat.

But Noah could not see what had happened on the earth, because the door was shut, and the only window was up in the roof. But he felt that the ark was no longer moving, and he knew that the water must have gone down. So, after waiting for a time, Noah opened a window, and let loose a bird called a raven. The raven has strong wings; and this raven flew round and round until the waters had gone down. The raven found a place to rest, and did not come back to the ark.

After Noah had waited several days, he sent out a dove; but the dove could not find any place to rest, so it flew back to the ark. Then Noah waited a week longer, and afterward he sent out the dove again. And at the evening, the dove came back to the ark, which was its home; and in its bill was a fresh leaf which it had picked off from an olive tree.

So Noah knew that the water had gone down enough to let the trees grow again. He waited another

The Dove Returns to Noah's Ark

week, and sent out the dove again; but this time the dove flew away and never came back. Noah knew that the earth was becoming dry again. So he took off a part of the roof, and looked out, and saw that there was dry land all around the ark, and the waters were no longer everywhere.

Noah had now lived in the ark a little more than a year, and he was glad to see the green land and the trees once more. And God said to Noah:

"Come out of the ark, with your wife, and your sons, and their wives, and all the living things that are with you in the ark."

So Noah opened the door of the ark, and came out with his family. The animals, and birds, and creeping things in the ark, came out also, and began again to bring life to the earth.

The first thing that Noah did when he came out of the ark, was to give thanks to God for saving all his family when the rest of the people on the earth were destroyed. He built an altar, and laid upon it an offering to the Lord, and gave himself and his family to God, and promised to do God's will.

And God was pleased with Noah's offering, and God said:

"I will not again destroy the earth on account of men, no matter how bad they may be. From this time no flood shall again cover the earth; but the seasons of spring and summer and fall and winter, shall remain without change. I give to you the earth; you shall be the rulers of the ground and of every living thing upon it."

Then God caused a rainbow to appear in the sky. He told Noah and his sons that whenever they or the people after them should see the rainbow, they should remember that God had placed it in the sky and over the clouds as a sign of his promise, that he would never again send a flood to destroy man from the earth.

So as often as we see the beautiful rainbow, we are to remember that it is the sign of God's promise to the world.

Comprehension Exercise

Complete the sentences using the words below.

Noah
Methuselah
Japheth
rainbow

1. Enoch had a son named

   _____.

2. _____ was told by God to build an ark.

3. After the flood was over, God caused a

   _____ to appear in the sky.

4. Noah had three sons named Shem, Ham, and

   _____.

3 The Tower That Was Never Finished

GENESIS 10:1—11:9

After the great flood, the family of Noah and those who came after him grew in number, until as the years went on, the earth began to be full of people once more. But there was one great difference between the people who had lived before the flood and those who lived after it. Before the flood, all the people stayed close together, so that very many lived in one land, and no one lived in other lands. After the flood families began to move from one place to another, seeking for themselves new homes. Some went one way, and some another, so that as the number of people grew, they covered much more of the earth than those who had lived before the flood.

This moving about was a part of God's plan to have the whole earth used by men, and not merely a small part of it. Then, too, a family who wished to serve God, and do right, could go away to another land if the people around them became evil.

From Mount Ararat, where the ark rested, many of the people moved southward into a country between two great rivers, the rivers Tigris and Euphrates. In this area, they built homes for themselves. They undertook to build a great city, which should rule all the peoples around them. They found that the soil in that country could be made into bricks; and that the bricks could be burned and made hard; so that it was easy to build houses to live in, and walls around their city.

And the people said to each other, "Let us build a great tower that shall stand on the earth and shall reach up to the sky; so that we may be kept together, and not scattered abroad on the earth."

So they began to build their great tower out of brick, which they piled up, one level above another. But God did not wish all the people on the earth to live close together, just as they had lived before the great flood. God knew that if they lived close together, the wicked people would lead the good people away from God, and all the world would become evil again, as it had been before the flood.

This was the way that God kept people from staying in one place. While they were building this great city and tower which they intended to rule the world, God caused their speech to change. At that time all men were speaking one language, so that everybody could understand what every other person said.

God caused men to change their language, perhaps not all at once, but by degrees, little by little. After a time, the people that belonged to one family found that they could not understand what the people of another family were saying, just as now Germans do not understand English, and French people cannot talk to Italians, until they have learned their different languages.

As people began to grow apart in their speech they moved away into other places, where the families speaking one language could understand each other. So the men who were building the city and the great tower could no longer understand each other's speech. They left the building without finishing it, and many of them went away into other lands. So the building stayed forever unfinished.

A city named Babel was built near the unfinished tower. The word babel means "confusion." It was afterward

Building the Tower of Babel

known as Babylon, and for a long time was one of the greatest cities of that part of the world, even after many of its people moved away.

Part of the people who left Babylon went up to the north and built a city called Nineveh, which became the ruling city of a great land called Assyria, whose people were called Assyrians.

Another company went away to the west and settled by the great river Nile, and founded the land of Egypt, with its strange temples and pyramids.

Another company wandered northwest until they came to the shore of the great sea which we call the Mediterranean Sea. There they founded the cities of Sidon and Tyre. Many of these people were sailors, sailing to countries far away, and bringing home many things from other lands to sell to the people of Babylon, Assyria, Egypt, and other countries.

So after the flood the earth again became covered with people, living in many lands and speaking many languages.

Comprehension Exercise

Complete the sentences using the words below.

whole
languages
tower
confusion

1. God wanted people to fill the

   _____ earth.

2. The wicked people at Babel started to build a

   _____.

3. The word "babel" means

   _____.

4. The people left their building project because God had changed their

   _____.

4 The Boy Who Became an Archer

GENESIS 21:1—21

Among the many cities which the people built were two called Sodom and Gomorrah. The people in these cities were very wicked and were nearly all destroyed. One good man named Lot and his family escaped. There was another good man named Abraham who did not live in these cities. He tried to do God's will and was promised a son to bring joy into his family.

After Sodom and Gomorrah were destroyed, Abraham and his wife, Sarah, moved their tent and their camp away from that part of the land. They went to live near a place called Gerar, in the southwest, not far from the Mediterranean Sea. And there at last, the child whom God had promised to Abraham and Sarah was born. Abraham was a hundred years old when this child was born.

They named this child Isaac, as the angel had told them he should be named. Abraham and Sarah were so happy to have a little boy, that after a time they gave a great feast and invited all the people to come and rejoice with them, and all in honor of the little Isaac.

Now Sarah had a maid named Hagar, an Egyptian woman. Hagar ran away from Sarah, her mistress, because Sarah mistreated her. An angel of the Lord found her by a well, and told her to go back to Sarah. Hagar had a child too, and his name was Ishmael. So now there were two boys in Abraham's tent, the older boy, Ishmael, the son of Hagar, and the younger boy, Isaac, the son of Abraham and Sarah.

Ishmael did not like the little Isaac, and did not treat him kindly. This made Sarah very angry, so she said to her husband.

"I do not wish to have this boy Ishmael growing up with my son Isaac. Send away Hagar and her boy, for they are a trouble to me."

Abraham felt very sorry that trouble had come between Sarah and Hagar, and between Isaac and Ishmael; for Abraham was a kind and good man, and he was friendly to them all.

But the Lord said to Abraham, "Do not be troubled about Ishmael and his mother. Do as Sarah has asked you to do, and send them away. It is best that Isaac should be left alone in your tent, for he is to receive everything that is yours. I the Lord will take care of Ishmael, and will make a great people of his descendants, those who shall come from him."

So the next morning Abraham sent Hagar and her boy away, expecting them to go back to the land of Egypt, from which Hagar had come. He gave them some food for the journey, and a bottle of water to drink by the way. The bottles in that country are not like ours, made of glass. They are made from the skin of a goat sewed tightly together. Abraham filled one of these skin-bottles with water and gave it to Hagar.

Hagar walked away from Abraham's tent, leading her little boy. However, after a short time she became lost, and wandered over the desert, not knowing where she was, until all the water in the bottle was used up. Her poor boy, in the hot sun and the burning sand, had nothing to drink. She thought that he would die of his terrible thirst. She laid him down under a little bush, then she went away. She said to herself:

Hagar Praying for Water

"I cannot bear to look at my poor boy dying for lack of water."

And just at that moment, while Hagar was crying, and her boy was moaning with thirst, she heard a voice saying to her: "Hagar, what is your trouble? Do not be afraid. God has heard your cry and the cry of your child. God will take care of you both, and will make of your boy a great nation of people."

It was the voice of an angel from heaven; and then Hagar looked, and there, close at hand, was a spring of water in the desert. How glad Hagar was as she filled the bottle with water and took it to her suffering boy under the bush!

After this Hagar did not go down to Egypt. She found a place where she could live and brought up her son in the wilderness, far from other people. God cared for Ishmael, and let him live a long life. Ishmael grew up in the desert and learned to shoot with the bow and arrow. He became a wild man, and his children after him grew up to be wild men also. They were the Arabians of the desert, who even to this day have never been ruled by any other people but wander through the desert, and live as they please. So Ishmael came to be the father of many people, and his descendants, the wild Arabians of the desert, are living unto this day in that land.

Ishmael the Archer

Comprehension Exercise

Complete the sentences using the words below.

Gomorrah
Ishmael
Abraham
Isaac

1. Sodom and

   _____ were two cities filled with wicked people.

2. Sarah had a little boy named

   _____ .

3. Hagar had a little boy named

   _____ .

4. _____ was one hundred years old when his son, Isaac was born.

5 How an Angel's Voice Saved a Boy's Life

GENESIS 22:1—23:20

You remember that in those times of which we are telling when men worshipped God, they built an altar of earth or of stone, and laid an offering upon it as a gift to God. The offering was generally a sheep, or a goat, or a young ox—some animal that was used for food. Such an offering was called "a sacrifice."

But the people who worshipped idols often did what seems to us very showy and very terrible. They thought that it would please their gods if they would offer, as a sacrifice, the most precious living things that were their own. They would foolishly take their own little children and kill them upon their altars as offerings to the gods of wood and stone. These were not really gods, but dead idols.

God wished to show Abraham and all his descendants, those who should come after him, that he was not pleased with offerings of living people, killed on altars. God decided to teach Abraham, so that he and his children after him would never forget it. Then at the same time he wished to see how faithful and obedient Abraham would be to his commands.

So God gave to Abraham a command which he did not mean to have obeyed, though this he did not tell to Abraham. He said:

"Take now your son, your only son Isaac, whom you love so greatly, and go to the land of Moriah, and there on a mountain that I will show you, offer him for a burnt-offering to me."

Though this command filled Abraham's heart with pain, yet he would not be as surprised to receive it as a father would in our day. Such offerings were very common among all those people in the land where Abraham lived. Abraham never, for one moment, doubted or disobeyed God's word. He knew that Isaac was the child whom God had promised, and that God had promised, too, that Isaac should have children, and that those coming from Isaac should be a great nation. He did not see how God could keep his promise with regard to Isaac, if Isaac should be killed as an offering; unless indeed God should raise him up from the dead afterward.

Nevertheless, Abraham began at once to obey God's command. He took two young men with him and an ass laden with wood for the fire. He went toward the mountain in the north, Isaac, his son, walking by his side. For two days they walked, sleeping under the trees at night in the open country. On the third day, Abraham saw the mountain far away. And as they drew near to the mountain Abraham said to the young men:

"Stay here with the ass, while I go up yonder mountain with Isaac to worship; and when we have worshipped, we will come back to you."

For Abraham believed that in some way God would bring back Isaac to life. He took the wood from the ass and placed it on Isaac, and they walked up the mountain together. As they were walking, Isaac said:

"Father, here is the wood, but where is the lamb for the offering?"

And Abraham said, "My son, God will provide himself a lamb for a burnt offering."

And they came to the place on the top of the mountain. There Abraham built an altar of stones and earth heaped up; and on it he placed the wood. Then he tied the hands and the feet of Isaac, and laid him on the altar. Abraham lifted up his hand, holding a knife to kill his son. Another moment longer and Isaac would be slain by his own father's hand.

But just at that moment the angel of the Lord called to Abraham, and said:

"Abraham! Abraham!"

"God Will Provide Himself a Lamb for a Burnt Offering."

And Abraham answered, "Here I am, Lord." Then the angel of the Lord said:

"Do not lay your hand upon your son. Do no harm to him. Now I know that you love God more than you love your only son, and that you are obedient to God, since you are ready to give up your son, your only son, to God."

What a relief and a joy these words from heaven brought to the heart of Abraham! How glad he was to know that it was not God's will for him to kill his son! Then Abraham looked around, and there in the thicket was a ram caught by his horns. And Abraham took the ram and offered him up for a burnt offering in place of his son. So Abraham's words came true when he said that God would provide for himself a lamb.

The place where this altar was built Abraham named Jehovah-jireh, which means, "The Lord will provide."

This offering, which seems so strange, did much good. It showed to Abraham, and to Isaac also, that Isaac belonged to God, for to God he had been offered; and in Isaac all those who should come from him, his descendants, had been given to God. It also showed to Abraham and to all the people after him, that God did not wish children or men killed as offerings for worship. Although the wicked people continued to offer such sacrifices, the Israelites, who came from Abraham and from Isaac, never offered them. They offered oxen and sheep and goats instead. This event also looked forward to a time when, just as Abraham gave his son as an offering, God should give his Son, Jesus Christ, to die for the sins of his people. All this was taught in this act of worship on Mount Moriah.

At this time Abraham was living at a place called Beersheba, on the border of the desert, south of the land of Canaan. From Beersheba he took

Abraham's Servant Meets Rebekah at the Well

this journey to Mount Moriah, and to Beersheba he came again after the offering on the mountain. Beersheba was the home of Abraham during most of his later years. After a time Sarah, the wife of Abraham and the mother of Isaac died, being one hundred and twenty years old. Abraham then bought, from the people at Hebron, a cave called the cave of Machpelah where he buried Sarah, his wife. This place is still known as the city of Hebron, but the people who live there will not allow any strangers to visit the cave.

Comprehension Exercise

Complete the sentences using the words below.

Isaac
Moriah
altars
Jehovah-jireh

1. People, like Abraham, offered sacrifice to God on stone

   _____.

2. God told Abraham to offer

   _____, his son as a sacrifice on a mountain.

3. The word "_____

   _____" means "The Lord will provide."

4. Abraham did not need to sacrifice his son on Mount

   _____.

6 How Jacob Gained His Brother's Blessing

GENESIS 25:27—27:46

After Abraham died, his son Isaac lived in the land of Canaan. Like his father, Isaac had his home in a tent. Many of his servants and friends also lived in tents. These people had many flocks of sheep and herds of cattle feeding wherever they could find grass to eat and water to drink.

Isaac and his wife Rebekah had two children. The older was named Esau and the younger Jacob. Esau was a man of the woods and fond of hunting; he was rough and covered with hair. Jacob was quiet and thoughtful, staying at home and caring for the flocks of his father. Isaac loved Esau more than Jacob, because Esau brought to his father that which he had killed in his hunting. However, Rebekah liked Jacob, because she saw that he was wise and careful in his work.

Among the people in those lands, when a man dies, his older son receives twice as much as the younger of what the father has owned. This was called his "birthright," for it was his right as the oldest born. So Esau, as the older, had a "birthright" to more of Isaac's possessions than Jacob. And besides this, there was the privilege of the promise of God that the family of Isaac should receive great blessings.

Now Esau, when he grew up, did not care for his birthright or the blessing which God had promised. But Jacob, who was a wise man, wished greatly to have the birthright which would come to Esau when his father died. Once, when Esau came home, hungry and tired from hunting in the fields, he saw that Jacob had a bowl of something that he had just cooked for dinner. And Esau said:

"Give me some of that red stuff in the dish. Will you not give me some? I am hungry."

And Jacob answered, "I will give it to you, if you will first of all sell to me your birthright."

And Esau said, "What is the use of the birthright to me now, when I am almost starving to death? You can have my birthright if you will give me something to eat."

Esau Sells His Birthright to Jacob

Then Esau made Jacob a solemn promise to give to Jacob his birthright, all for a bowl of food. It was not right for Jacob to deal so selfishly with his brother, but it was very wrong for Esau to care so little for his birthright and God's blessing.

Some time after this, when Esau was forty years old, he married two wives. Though this would be very wicked in our times, it was not supposed to be wrong then; for even good men then had more than one wife. But Esau's two wives were women from the people of Canaan, who worshipped idols, and not the true God. And they taught their children also to pray to idols, so that those who came from Esau, the people who were his descendants, lost all knowledge of God, and became very wicked. This sad process of events took place over many years.

Isaac and Rebekah were very sorry to have their son, Esau, marry women who prayed to idols and not to God, but still Isaac loved his active son, Esau, more than his quiet son, Jacob. But Rebekah loved Jacob more than she did Esau.

Isaac became very old and feeble, and so blind that he could hardly see anything. One day he said to Esau:

"My son, I am very old, and do not know how soon I must die. But before I die, I wish to give to you, as my older son, God's blessing upon you, and your children, and your descendants. Go out into the fields, and with your bow and arrows shoot some animal that is good for food, and make for me a dish of cooked meat such as you know I love; and after I have eaten it I will give you the blessing."

Now Esau ought to have told his father that the blessing did not belong to him, for he had sold it to his brother Jacob. But he did not tell his father. He went out into the fields hunting, to find the kind of meat which his father liked the most.

Now Rebekah was listening, and heard all that Isaac had said to Esau. She knew that it would be better for Jacob to have the blessing than for Esau. She loved Jacob more than Esau. So she called to Jacob and told him what Isaac had said to Esau, and she said:

"Now, my son, do what I tell you, and you will get the blessing instead of your brother. Go to the flocks and bring to me two little kids from the goats, and I will cook them just like the meat which Esau cooks for your father. And you will bring it to your father, and he will think that you are Esau, and will give you the blessing; it really belongs to you."

But Jacob said, "You know that Esau and I are not alike. His neck and

arms are covered with hairs, while mine are smooth. My father will feel me, and he will find that I am not Esau. Instead of giving me a blessing, I am afraid that he will curse me."

But Rebekah answered her son, "Never mind, you do as I have told you, and I will take care of you. If any harm comes it will come to me; so do not be afraid, but go and bring the meat."

Then Jacob went and brought a pair of little kids from the flocks, and from them his mother made a dish of food, so that it would be to the taste just as Isaac liked it. Then Rebekah found some of Esau's clothes, and dressed Jacob in them. She placed on his neck and his hands some of the skins of the kids, so that his neck and his hands would feel rough and hairy to the touch.

Then Jacob came into his father's tent, bringing the dinner, and speaking as much like Esau as he could, he said: "Here I am, my father."

And Isaac said, "Who are you, my son?"

And Jacob answered, "I am Esau, your oldest son; I have done as you bade me, now sit up and eat the dinner that I have made, and then give

"Now my son, do what I tell you."

Isaac Blessing Jacob

me your blessing as you promised me."

And Isaac said, "How is it that you found it so quickly?" Jacob answered, "Because the Lord your God showed me where to go and gave me good success."

Isaac did not feel certain that it was his son Esau, and he said, Come near and let me feel you, so that I may know that you are really my son Esau."

And Jacob went up close to Isaac's bed, and Isaac felt his face, and his neck, and his hands, and he said: "The voice sounds like Jacob, but the hands are the hands of Esau. "Are you really my son Esau?"

And Jacob told a lie to his father, and said "I am."

Then the old man ate the food that Jacob had brought to him, then he kissed Jacob, believing him to be Esau, and he gave the blessing to him, saying:

"May God give you the dew of heaven, and the richness of the earth, and plenty of grain and wine. May nations bow down to you and peoples become your servants. May you be the master over your brother, and may your family and descendants that shall come from you rule over his family and his descendants. Blessed be those that bless you, and cursed be those that curse you."

Just as soon as Jacob had received the blessing he rose up and hastened away. He had scarcely gone out, when Esau came in from hunting, with the dish of food that he had cooked. And he said:

"Let my father sit up and eat the food that I have brought, and give me the blessing."

And Isaac said, "Why, who are you?"

Esau answered, "I am your son; your oldest son, Esau."

And Isaac trembled and said, "Who then is the one that came in and brought to me food? and I have eaten his food and have blessed him; yes, and he shall be blessed."

When Esau heard this, he knew that he had been cheated, and he cried aloud, with a bitter cry, "O, my father, my brother has taken away my blessing, just as he took away my birthright! But cannot you give me another blessing, too? Have you given everything to my brother?"

And Isaac told him all that he had said to Jacob, making him the ruler over his brother.

But Esau begged for another blessing, and Isaac said:

"My son, your dwelling shall be of the riches of the earth and of the dew of heaven. You shall live by your sword and your descendants shall serve his descendants. But in time to come they shall break loose and shall shake off the yoke of your brother's rule and shall be free."

All this came to pass many years afterward. The people who came from Esau lived in a land called Edom, on the south of the land of Israel, where Jacob's descendants lived. After a time, the Israelites became rulers over the Edomites; and later still, the Edomites made themselves free from the Israelites. But all this took place hundreds of years after both Esau and Jacob had died. The blessing of God's covenant or promise came to Israel, and not to the people from Esau.

It was better that Jacob's descendants, those who came after him, should have the blessing, than that Esau's people should have it; for Jacob's people worshipped God, and Esau's people walked in the darkness of sin and became wicked.

Comprehension Exercise

Complete the sentences using the words below.

Rebekah
Esau
Israel
Canaan

1. Isaac lived in the land of

   _____.

2. _____ sold his birthright to Jacob for some food.

3. Isaac had a wife named

   _____.

4. God established his covenant

   with _____.

7 Jacob's Wonderful Dream

GENESIS 27:46—30:24

After Esau found that he had lost his birthright and his blessing, he was very angry against his brother Jacob. He said to himself, and told others, "My father Isaac is very old and cannot live long. As soon as he is dead, then I shall kill Jacob for having robbed me of my right."

When Rebekah heard this, she said to Jacob, "Before it is too late, you must go away from home and get out of Esau's sight. Perhaps when Esau sees you no longer, he will forget his anger, and then you can come home again. Go and visit my brother Laban, your uncle, in Haran, and stay with him for a little while."

We must remember that Rebekah came from the family of Nahor, Abraham's younger brother, who lived in Haran, a long distance to the northeast of Canaan.

So Jacob went out of Beersheba, on the border of the desert, and walked alone, carrying his staff in his hand. One evening, just about sunset, he came to a place among the mountains, more than sixty miles away from his home. And as he had no bed to lie down upon, he took a stone and rested his head upon it for a pillow, and lay down to sleep.

During the night, Jacob had a wonderful dream. In his dream, he saw stairs leading from the earth where he lay up to heaven; angels were going up and coming down upon the stairs. And above the stairs, he saw the Lord God standing. And God said to Jacob:

"I am the Lord, the God of Abraham, and the God of Isaac your father, and I will be your God, too. The land where you are lying all alone, shall belong to you and to your children after you, and your children shall spread abroad over the lands, east and west, and north and south like the dust of the earth; and in your family all the world shall receive a blessing. And I am with you in your journey, and I will keep you where you are going, and will bring you back to this land. I will never leave you, and I will surely keep my promise to you."

AND HE DREAMED,

AND BEHOLD A

SET UP ON THE

AND THE TOP

OF IT REACHED

AND BEHOLD THE

TO

OF GOD ASCENDING

AND DESCENDING ON IT.

GENESIS 28:12

And in the morning Jacob awakened from his sleep, and he said:

"Surely, the Lord is in this place, and I did not know it! I thought that I was all alone, but God has been with me. This place is the house of God; it is the gate of heaven!"

And Jacob took the stone on which his head had rested, and he set it up as a pillar, and poured oil on it as an offering to God. And Jacob named that place Bethel, which in the language that Jacob spoke means "The House of God."

And Jacob made a promise to God at that time, and said, "If God really will go with me and will keep me in the way that I go, and will give me bread to eat and will bring me to my father's house in peace, then the Lord shall be my God and this stone shall be the house of God, and of all that God gives me I will give back to God one-tenth as an offering."

Then Jacob went onward in his long journey. He walked across the river Jordan in a shallow place, feeling the way with his staff. He climbed mountains and journeyed beside the great desert on the east. Finally, he came to the city of Haran. Beside the city was the well, where Abraham's servant had met Jacob's mother, Rebekah, and there, after Jacob had waited for a time, he saw a young woman coming with her sheep to give them water.

Then Jacob took off the flat stone that was over the mouth of the well, and drew water and gave it to the sheep. He soon found out that this young woman was his own cousin Rachel, the daughter of Laban. Jacob was so glad that he wept for joy. At that moment, he began to love Rachel, and longed to have her for his wife.

Rachel's father, Laban, who was Jacob's uncle, gave a welcome to Jacob, and took him into his home.

And Jacob asked Laban if he would give his daughter, Rachel, to him as his wife. Jacob said, "If you give me Rachel, I will work for you seven years."

And Laban said, "It is better that you should have her, than that a stranger should marry her."

So Jacob lived seven years in Laban's house, caring for his sheep and oxen and camels; and such was his love for Rachel that the seven years seemed like a few days.

At last the day came for the marriage. They brought in the bride, who, after the manner of that land, was covered with a thick veil, so that her face could not be seen. And she was married to Jacob, and when Jacob lifted up her veil he found that he had married, not Rachel whom he loved, but her older sister, Leah. Jacob did not love this woman at all.

Jacob was very angry that he had been deceived, though that was just the way in which Jacob himself had deceived his father and cheated his brother Esau. But his uncle Laban said:

"In our land we never allow the younger daughter to be married before the older daughter. Keep Leah for your wife, and work for me seven years longer, and you shall have Rachel also."

For in those times, as we have seen, men often had two wives, or even more than two. No one thought that it was wrong then to have more than one wife; although now it is considered very foolish. So Jacob stayed seven years more, fourteen years in all, before he received Rachel as his wife.

While Jacob was living at Haran, eleven sons were born to him. But only one of these was the child of Rachel, whom Jacob loved. This son was Joseph, who was dearer to Jacob than his other children. Jacob was no longer a young father and therefore he considered Joseph to be a special son.

Comprehension Exercise

Complete the sentences using the words below.

| Rachel |
| Laban |
| Leah |
| Bethel |

1. Jacob left his home to visit his uncle,

   _____.

2. Jacob met his cousin,

   _____, at the well.

3. The word

   "_____"
   means "The House of God."

4. Jacob was first married to

   _____ by way of a special trick.

8 A Midnight Wrestling Match

GENESIS 30:25—33:20

Jacob stayed a long time in the land of Haran, much longer than he had expected to stay. At last, after twenty years, Jacob decided to go back to the land of Canaan, and to his father Isaac, who was still living, though now very old and feeble. By God's grace, Jacob had become rich in the land of Haran.

Jacob did not tell his uncle Laban that he was going away; but while Laban was absent from home, Jacob gathered together his wives, and children, and all his sheep and cattle, and he went away quietly. When Laban found that Jacob had left him, he was not at all pleased. He wanted Jacob to still care for the things that he owned, for, Jacob managed them better than Laban himself. God blessed everything that Jacob undertook. Then, too, Laban did not like

to have his two daughters, the wives of Jacob, taken so far away from him.

So Laban and the men who were with him followed after Jacob; but that night God spoke to Laban in a dream, and said:

"Do no harm to Jacob when you meet him." Therefore, when Laban came to where Jacob was in his camp on Mount Gilead, on the east of the river Jordan, Laban spoke kindly to Jacob. And Jacob and Laban made a covenant; that is, a promise between them. They piled up a heap of stones; and on it they set up a large rock like a pillar; and beside the heap of stones, they ate a meal together; and Jacob said to Laban:

"I promise not to go past this heap of stones and this pillar to do you any harm. The God of your grandfather Nahor, and the God of my grandfather Abraham, be the judge between us."

Laban made the same promise to Jacob; and then he kissed his daughters, and all of Jacob's children, and told them good-bye. Laban went back to Haran, and Jacob went on to Canaan.

And Jacob gave two names to the heap of stones where they had made the covenant. One name was "Gilead," a word which means "The Heap of Witness"; the other was "Mizpah," which means "Watch-tower." For Jacob said, "The Lord watch between you and me, when we are absent from each other."

While Jacob was going back to Canaan, he heard news that filled him with fear. He heard that Esau, his brother, was coming to meet him, leading an army of four hundred men. He knew how angry Esau had been long before and how he had threatened to kill him. Jacob feared that Esau would now come upon him, and kill not only himself, but his wives and his children. If Jacob had acted rightly toward his brother, he need not have feared Esau's coming, but he knew how he had wronged Esau while at home with their father.

That night Jacob divided his company into two parts; so that if one part were taken, the other part might escape. And he sent onward before him as a present to his brother a great drove of oxen and cows, and sheep and goats, and camels and asses, hoping that by the present his brother might be made more kind toward him.

And then Jacob prayed earnestly to the Lord God to help him. After that he sent all his family across a brook that was in his path, called the brook Jabbok, while he stayed alone on the other side of the brook to pray again.

And while Jacob was alone, he felt that a man had taken hold of him, and Jacob wrestled with this strange man all the night. The man was an angel from God. They wrestled so hard, that Jacob's thigh was strained in the struggle. And the angel said:

"Let me go, for the day is breaking."

And Jacob said: "I will not let thee go, until thou hast blessed me."

Then the angel said, "What is your name?"

And Jacob answered, "Jacob is my name."

Then the angel said: "Your name shall no more be called Jacob, but Israel; that is, 'He who wrestles with God.' For you have wrestled with God and have won the victory."

The angel blessed him there. And the sun rose as the angel left him, and Jacob gave a name to that place. He called it Peniel, or Penuel, words which in the language that Jacob spoke mean "The Face of God." "For," said Jacob, "I have met God face to face."

After this fight Jacob was lame; for in the wrestle, he had strained his thigh.

And as Jacob went across the brook Jabbok early in the morning, he looked up, and there was Esau right before him. He bowed with his face to the ground, over and over again, as people do in those lands when they meet someone of higher rank than their own. But Esau ran to meet him, and placed his arms around his neck, and kissed him; and the two brothers wept together. Esau was kind and generous to forgive his brother all the wrong that he had done and at first he would not receive Jacob's present, for he said, I have enough, my brother." But Jacob urged him, until at last he took the present. Thankfully, the quarrel was ended, and the two brothers were at peace.

Jacob came to Shechem, in the middle of the land of Canaan, and there he set up his tents. At the foot of the mountain, although there were streams of water all around, he dug his own well, great and deep. This same well was used by Jesus many years later, and the well may still be seen. Even now the traveler who visits that place may drink water from Jacob's well.

After this Jacob had a new name, Israel, which means, as we have seen, "The one who wrestles with God." Sometimes he was called Jacob, and sometimes Israel. And all those who came from Israel, his descendants, were called Israelites.

After this Isaac died, very old, and was buried by his sons Jacob and Esau in the cave at Hebron, where Abraham and Sarah were buried already. Esau, with his children and his cattle, went away to a land on the southeast of Canaan, which was called Edom. And Jacob, or Israel, and his family lived in the land of Canaan, dwelling in tents, and moving from place to place, where they could find good pasture, or grass upon which to feed their flocks.

Comprehension Exercise

Complete the sentences using the words below.

Israel
Esau
angel
Hebron

1. Jacob was afraid to meet his brother

   _____.

2. An _____
   wrestled with Jacob all night.

3. Jacob was given the new name

   of _____ by
   God's angel.

4. Isaac was buried in a cave at

   _____.

9 The Story of Joseph and His Brothers

GENESIS 37:1—47:31

Joseph's Sheaf Stands Upright

Jacob lived in the land of Canaan many years and the Lord blessed him with another son named Benjamin. The ten oldest sons of Jacob were kept busy, working in the fields, raising wheat, and seeing that their father's sheep and cattle had plenty of grass and grain to eat. But the two youngest sons stayed closer to the father's tent. These two youngest sons of Rachel and Jacob were named Joseph and Benjamin.

Now Jacob loved Joseph better than he loved any of his other children. And because he loved him so dearly, he gave him a wonderful coat. It was soft and beautiful, and it had many different colors. Not one of Joseph's brothers had a coat anything like it. When they slept out in the fields, his ten older brothers had nothing to wear but coarse, hairy goatskins. When they were at home in their tents, they had nothing to put on but long, loose cotton shirts which they slipped on over their heads. It made all of them very angry to see their younger brother Joseph walking about in his handsome coat of many colors. They did not like to be reminded that their father loved Joseph best.

There were other reasons why the older brothers hated Joseph. They sometimes did wicked and cruel things, and Joseph, who was usually good and kind, would not join them. Besides, they did not like the dreams Joseph had.

Once, Joseph dreamed that he and his brothers were in the fields binding the wheat into big bundles. These bundles were called sheaves.

In Joseph's dream a very strange thing happened. His sheaf of wheat stood up straight and tall, and his brothers' sheaves all lay down flat on the ground before it. When Joseph told his brothers this dream they were very angry. "Does this boy think we are going to bow down to him and obey him? "they asked one another.

Then Joseph had another dream. He dreamed that the sun and the moon and eleven stars bowed down before him, as though he were a great man.

When Joseph told this dream to his father and his brothers, Joseph's father thought that the sun and the moon in Joseph's dream meant himself and Joseph's mother. He also thought that the eleven stars meant Joseph's brothers.

Jacob wondered how a shepherd boy like Joseph would ever become a great man. But the brothers asked one another, "Shall Joseph some day be like a king and rule over us?" And after that they hated him more than ever.

One morning Joseph started out to find his brothers. They had traveled a long way from home to find fresh fields and watering places for the sheep and cattle. They had been away such a long time that their father, Jacob, wanted to hear from them. He wished to know if they were well, and if they and their sheep and cattle were getting enough to eat. And so he sent Joseph to find out.

Joseph obeyed his father and started on his journey. He put on his beautiful coat of many colors. It was not the best kind of a covering for a long walk, but he liked to wear it.

When Joseph reached Shechem, the place where he expected to find his brothers, they had moved on to find new fields and wells. Someone told Joseph which way they had gone, and he walked and walked until he found them.

The brothers saw Joseph coming. "Let us kill him," they said. "We can tell our father that a wild beast has killed him." Only anger and hate were in their hearts. They did not care even for their poor father's sorrow. One brother, Reuben, was kinder than the others. He wanted to save Joseph and take him back to his father. But there was only one Reuben and there were nine rough, sinful brothers. All Reuben could do was to make them promise not to kill Joseph just then. "We will put him into a deep hole," they said. "It is so deep that he cannot get out. There he can stay until he starves." Reuben

Joseph's Coat is Torn from Him

agreed. He meant to go back later, alone, and get Joseph out of the pit.

As soon as Joseph came up to their tents, the nine foolish brothers took hold of him and tore his beautiful coat from him. Then they threw him into the deep pit. After that, they sat down and ate their dinner.

As they were eating, a caravan stopped at their well. This caravan was a long line of camels, donkeys, and men and women on their way to a country called Egypt.

"Let us sell Joseph to them," said one of the brothers. The other brothers thought this was a good plan. After all, they really did not want to kill Joseph, and if he were sold to these people he would be taken a long way off. Then he couldn't bother them any more by

walking about in his grand coat and telling his strange dreams. They ran to the deep hole and pulled out Joseph.

"Will you buy a slave?" they asked the leader of the caravan. The man counted out twenty shiny silver pieces. These he gave to the brothers, who put them into the little bags they always carried inside their belts. Then the man took Joseph, and the caravan started away toward Egypt.

After the caravan had left, the cruel brothers killed a little goat and stained Joseph's many-colored coat with its blood. Then they went home to their father Jacob. They held up the coat, all torn and bloody. "This, we found," they said. "Is it not Joseph's coat?" "It is my son's

"Is it my son's coat?"

coat," said Jacob. "An evil beast hath devoured him."

Then Jacob tore his own coat in sorrow and put ashes on his head. No one could comfort him. "I will go down into the grave unto my son mourning," he said. And he wept for Joseph.

The hard-hearted brothers let their father believe that Joseph had been killed by a wild beast. They let him mourn for his favorite son. But they knew that Joseph was alive and on his way to the far-off land of Egypt.

10 Joseph in Egypt

As soon as the caravan reached Egypt, Joseph was sold to Potiphar, one of the king's officers. Potiphar did not put Joseph to work in the fields, but gave him work to do in the house. Joseph seemed to know the best way to do everything. He did so well that Potiphar made him manager of his house and of his fields.

Then a very unhappy thing happened. Potiphar's wife told false stories about Joseph. When Potiphar heard these stories, he grew angry with Joseph and put him in prison.

The jailer watched Joseph. He saw that the other prisoners were happier and worked more willingly when Joseph was near. "God must be with this boy," the jailer thought. So he put Joseph in charge of the other prisoners.

In the same prison with Joseph was the butler of Pharaoh, the king. One night this butler had a strange dream.

It worried him. He decided that he would ask Joseph if he could figure out what it meant. Joseph listened very carefully.

Pressing the Grapes into the King's Cup

"In my dream," the butler said, "behold, a vine was before me; and in the vine were three branches: and it budded, and her blossoms shot forth; and the clusters thereof brought forth ripe grapes: And Pharaoh's cup was in my hand: and I took the grapes, and pressed them into Pharaoh's cup, and I gave the cup into Pharaoh's hand."

"The three branches are three days," Joseph told him. "Within three days you will leave the prison, and become the king's butler again and give him his cup of wine, just as you did before. And when it is well with you again, I pray you make mention of me unto Pharaoh, the king. For indeed I was stolen out of the land of the Hebrews, and here also have I

Joseph is Shut up in Prison

all his servants. And he restored the butler to his place again, just as Joseph had said. But the butler did not think to tell the king about Joseph. As soon as he reached Pharaoh's palace, he forgot all about his friend in prison.

Joseph felt sure that the butler would remember him.

done nothing that they should put me into the dungeon."

Three days later was the king's birthday, and Pharaoh made a feast for

Every day, after the butler had left the prison, Joseph must have gone to the window to watch for him. For two years Joseph waited. Then one day men came to the prison and called for Joseph. They told him that Pharaoh, the king, wanted to see him. "Pharaoh has had a dream," they said, "and you are to try to tell him what it means." The butler had at last remembered Joseph!

It would not do to keep the king waiting. Neither would it do to appear before him in jail clothes. So Joseph washed himself, and put on fresh clothes, and hurried to the king's palace.

Watching for the Butler's Return

Pharaoh told Joseph that no one, not even the wisest men of Egypt, could tell him the meaning of what he had dreamed. But because Joseph had told the butler the meaning of his dream, and it had happened as he had said, the king had sent for him.

This was Pharaoh's dream. As he stood by a river, he saw seven fine, fat cows come up out of the water. Behind them came seven lean, sickly cows. These lean cows ate up the fat ones, but then they were still leaner than they were before.

Joseph told the king that the seven fat cows meant seven years of plenty, and that the seven lean cows meant seven years of famine. Egypt would have seven good years, with plenty of food for everyone, and then there would come a dreadful famine that would last seven years. There would be no rain, and every-

The Fat and Lean Cows

thing green would die. The people would all go hungry.

"What can we do?" the troubled king asked Joseph.

"In the seven years of plenty," Joseph said, "while there is enough for everyone, food can be saved for the years of famine. Raise wheat and still more wheat. Build great storehouses and fill them full of grain. Every kind of food that can be packed away should be put into the storehouses. Then, when the long famine time comes, the people of Egypt will have enough to eat."

Seven Years of Plenty

Pharaoh was pleased with Joseph's plan. It would need a wise man to see about the raising of grain, and the building of storehouses and filling them with food. Pharaoh thought Joseph would be just the man. So he made Joseph ruler over Egypt, next to himself. The king gave him rich clothes, put a gold chain around his neck, and took the ring from his own finger and put it onto Joseph's finger.

Joseph was now a great man. He lived in a big house, wore fine clothes, and rode in a handsome chariot, right after the king. Everyone bowed down before him and obeyed him. For seven years he looked after the raising of food and storing it away. Then came the famine.

11 Joseph Forgives His Brothers

So much food had been stored up in Egypt during the years of plenty that, when famine came, there was enough for the Egyptians, as Joseph had planned. But people of other countries had not been so wise. They had not saved their wheat. Now they came to Egypt to buy food. Joseph managed this, too, keeping enough for the people of Egypt, and selling what could be spared to those who came from other lands.

In the country of Canaan, not far from Egypt, Joseph's father, Jacob who was now very old, was growing very hungry because of the famine. His eleven sons who lived near him were hungry, too, and their wives and children. There was little food for them to eat, and there was no grass or hay for their cattle and sheep to feed on.

Jacob had heard that there was a great man in Egypt who was selling food to hungry people. He did not imagine that this great man was his own son Joseph. He and his sons and their families must have food at once or they would starve. So Jacob sent his sons, except the youngest one, Benjamin, down to Egypt to buy food for them all and grain for their cattle and sheep. These ten sons were the same wicked brothers who had sold Joseph into Egypt. But they had forgotten all about that. As they journeyed toward Egypt they thought only about the food they were going to buy. They had many empty sacks on the backs of their donkeys and plenty of money in their money belts.

When they reached Egypt, they went to Joseph's palace. There the ten brothers asked to see the man who could sell them food. As they came into the room where Joseph was, they bowed themselves down to the floor in front of him. Here were Joseph's hungry brothers kneeling before him, and begging him to sell them food. Joseph knew them at once, but they did not know him.

As Joseph looked at them he remembered his dream of long ago. He remembered how all his brothers' sheaves of wheat had lain flat on the ground before his sheaf. His dream had at last come true!

At first Joseph was not glad to see his brothers. But he wanted to hear about his father, Jacob, and his

Joseph's Brothers Lie Flat Before Him

youngest brother, Benjamin, whom he had always loved. So he asked the men kneeling before him about their homes and families. Then he pretended to believe that they had not come to Egypt to buy food at all, but to see how bad things were in Egypt, because of the famine. They told Joseph that they were not spies, but that they were ten brothers. Their youngest brother, they said, was at home with their father.

"If what you say is true," Joseph answered, "bring your youngest brother to me. Then I shall see that you are truthful men." But he let them fill their sacks with grain, and start back with their heavily loaded donkeys. And he told men to put into the sacks the money that the brothers had paid for the grain.

When the brothers were part way home, they opened their sacks to get grain for the donkeys. Every man found his bag of money in his sack. Joseph had made them a present of the grain. At first the brothers were frightened, for they thought that something was wrong. They thought of going back, but their families needed the food so much that they kept on toward home.

They told their father all that had happened to them. "The man, the lord of Egypt, spoke roughly with us, and took us for spies," they told Jacob. "And the lord of Egypt said,

Finding the Money in the Grain Sacks

'Bring your youngest brother to me. Then I shall know that ye are not spies.'"

Jacob was very sad. "Joseph is gone, he said, "and now you want to take Benjamin away. Why did you tell the man that you had a brother at home?"

And the brothers answered, "The man asked us, 'Is your father yet alive? Have ye another brother?' And we told him. Could we know that he would say, 'Bring your brother down to Egypt?' "

Jacob was a rich man. He and his sons had plenty of money, but that did not help Jacob now. There was no wheat or corn to be bought in Canaan, where Jacob lived. It was only in Egypt that there was any food to buy. But Jacob did not want his sons to go back to Egypt for more grain, because they must take Benjamin with them. "The lord of Egypt who sells the grain told us he would not see us again unless Benjamin came with us," the brothers said.

But when there was no more wheat or corn left, and all of Jacob's big family was hungry again, Jacob knew that he must let Benjamin go. He prepared a present of spices and nuts and fruits for his sons to give to the great man of Egypt. And he told

them to take twice as much money as they had taken before, besides the money that had been returned to them in their grain sacks.

As soon as the brothers reached Egypt, they hurried to Joseph's palace.

When Joseph saw that Benjamin, his well-loved brother, was with the brothers, he made a great feast for them. And he gave them all they could eat, but he gave Benjamin more than any of the rest.

Then Joseph could not keep silent any longer. "I am Joseph, your brother," he said, "whom ye sold into Egypt."

The brothers could not answer; they were afraid. But Joseph told them

Joseph Forgives His Brothers

that he forgave them everything. He said that he longed to see his father, and that he wanted to keep Benjamin with him. "The famine will last five more years," he said. "Bring my father to Egypt, and come yourselves and bring your families, and your sheep and cattle, too. Live near me, and I will see that you all have plenty to eat and do not lack anything."

And then Joseph kissed Benjamin, and wept with joy at being with him again. And he kissed all his brothers. And they talked together for a long time.

By this time everyone in Joseph's palace knew that Joseph's brothers were with him. Someone even told Pharaoh, and it pleased him.

"Tell your brothers," Pharaoh sent word to Joseph, "that they and their families and their father are welcome in Egypt. Have them take back plenty of food, and wagons too, so that they may bring your, father and their wives and children here in comfort."

So the brothers went back to Canaan. What excitement there must have been when they told Jacob their wonderful news! Joseph was alive! Joseph was the great man of Egypt! Joseph had invited them all to come to Egypt to live!

At first Jacob could hardly believe the news. But his sons told him everything that Joseph had said. And they gave him the presents Joseph had sent him, and showed him the wagons Pharaoh had sent for Jacob and the others to ride in, back to Egypt. Then Jacob believed them, and he said, "Joseph my son is yet alive: I will go and see him before I die."

And they strapped the tents onto the camels and donkeys. They drove the sheep and cattle before them. Jacob and the mothers and little children rode in the wagons.

The Journey into Egypt

And so they went to the land of Egypt–Jacob and all his sons and their families☐to live near Joseph. The Lord truly blessed Jacob and thousands of hungry people through the good work of Joseph.

Comprehension Exercise

Complete the sentences using the words below.

Egypt
Pharaoh
Jacob
Joseph

1. Jacob's two youngest sons were named

   _____ and Benjamin.

2. Joseph was sold as a slave and sent off to

   _____.

3. Joseph told the

   _____ that a famine was coming to Egypt in seven years.

4. _____ and his sons went to Egypt with their families.

12 The Story of Moses

EXODUS 1:1—2:22

Pharaoh, the king of Egypt, had told Joseph to have his father Jacob, and his eleven brothers and all their families come to live in Egypt.

"You need never go back to Canaan," the king told them. "There is plenty of room in Egypt for you."

About seventy of these relatives of Joseph came to live near him in the land of Pharaoh. By and by, as there were more grandchildren and great-grandchildren of Jacob, there were hundreds of them. These people who were descendants of Jacob were called Hebrews.

Everything went well as long as Joseph lived, and the king who was his friend. But after that king died there were other kings of Egypt who were not so kind. At last, many years after Joseph's death, there was a king of Egypt who wanted the country just for the Egyptians. He forgot that the Hebrew people had been invited to come to Egypt, and he treated them like slaves. Instead of making them feel welcome, as the Pharaoh who was Joseph's friend had done, he was cruel to them. He made them work very hard, making bricks and building storehouses for him. This Pharaoh wanted to keep the Hebrews in Egypt, but he did not want them to have any power.

But God was with the Hebrews, and He made them so strong that even the hard work that Pharaoh, the king, made them do did not hurt them. They grew into a powerful people, so powerful that Pharaoh became afraid of them.

"What shall we do with these Hebrews?" the king asked his soldiers. "They will soon be stronger than we Egyptians are. Then they may join our enemies and make war on us. They might even take our country from us and rule over it themselves." And when the soldiers had no answer, the king said, "I will order all the Hebrew boy babies to be drowned. Then they can never grow up to be soldiers and fight against me." So the wicked king ordered all the Hebrew boy babies to be drowned in the river.

There was one Hebrew mother who did not intend to have her baby boy drowned. She hid him in her tiny hut, and she kept him from crying or making any noise. No Egyptian imagined that there was a baby in that little home, everything was so quiet. But the baby was growing every day, and his mother could not hide him from the Egyptians any longer. What could she do? She prayed to God, and asked Him to help her save her baby. And then she went to work herself to try to save him.

Squatting on the floor of her mud hut, she wove a basket. She made it of coarse, strong reeds which grew on the river bank. And she covered it inside and out with a sticky pitch, so no water could get into it.

The baby had an older sister, Miriam. When her mother had finished weaving the basket and covering it with pitch, Miriam helped her look along the river for a safe place to put it. They were going to hide the baby in his water cradle among the tall, thick reeds.

Early one morning they carried the baby down to the river. He was fast asleep. It was so early that no one was walking along the river bank. They slid the basket, with the baby in it, into the water. There were tall green reeds all about it. The mother went back to her little home. But Miriam hid herself among the tall grasses and watched.

Soon something happened. A beautiful princess, who was the daughter of the wicked king, came down to the river for her morning bath.

"What a strange place for such a pretty basket!" she said to her maids, when she saw the basket at the edge of the water. "Bring it to me."

Imagine the princess' surprise when she opened the basket and found a baby in it!

"This is one of the Hebrews' children," the princess said. And she thought sadly of her father's cruel

Hiding the Basket Among the Reeds

order. "I will save him," she told her maids. "I will take care of him, and keep him as my son."

Miriam was very happy to see the beautiful princess holding her tiny brother in her arms. She came out of her hiding place. "Shall I get you a nurse for him?" she asked.

"Go," the princess told her, "and find a woman to care for the child."

Straight home to her mother Miriam ran. What excitement there was in that little home as she told her mother what had happened! "Come quickly, Mother!" Miriam said. "The princess has found the baby and she wants a nurse for him."

So it was his own mother who nursed and cared for the little Hebrew baby. Then, when he was old enough, he went to the king's palace and lived there as if he were the princess' own son.

And because the princess had found him in the water, and had drawn him out of it, she named him Moses, which means "drawn out."

Moses lived in the palace for many years. He had, for teachers, learned men who taught him much of the wisdom of ancient Egypt. And he had the finest kind of food and clothing and whatever else he wished. But he never forgot his own people. Whenever he saw the Egyptians being cruel to the Hebrew people, it made him sad. He made up his mind that some day he would help end their troubles and bring back happiness to the Hebrews.

13 Leaving Egypt

EXODUS 3:1—15:22

Pharaoh and the Egyptians may have thought that the Hebrews had no friends. But they were mistaken. The Hebrews had the greatest friend in all the world. That friend was God. Besides, there was the Hebrew, Moses, who had been rescued by the princess and who had grown up in Pharaoh's palace. God spoke to Moses. He told him to take the Hebrew people out of Egypt, and to lead them back into Canaan, where He would give them a beautiful country for their own. At first the Hebrew people were afraid. They would have to cross a wilderness before they could reach this country.

The Hebrews did not start at once. First Moses asked permission of the wicked king for them to leave. Sometimes Pharaoh told him that the Hebrew people might go. Then, just as soon as they were ready to start, he would tell Moses that the Hebrews must stay. Finally, God told Moses that it was time for them to go.

Moses told the Hebrew people to get ready. Just as soon as the signal came, they must start. God had told Moses what that signal would be. He had told Moses to warn Pharaoh that at midnight, in every Egyptian house, someone would die. Moses told the Hebrew people that when that dreadful thing happened, they were to leave at once.

"Sprinkle the blood of a lamb on your doors," Moses told them. "Those blood stains will show that you are God's people, and in your houses no one will die."

At midnight there was crying and mourning in every Egyptian house. But in the Hebrew homes there was no weeping. When Pharaoh learned that God had spared the children of the Hebrews, he decided that they must be God's people, and he did not dare keep them any longer from leaving Egypt. So he sent word to Moses that the Hebrew people should go.

"It is time to go!" Moses told his people. And a long line of cattle, sheep, goats, men, women, and children started their march eastward across the deserts and flat country toward the shores of the Red Sea.

No sooner were the Hebrews out of sight than Pharaoh began to wish

The Hebrews Gather Together Their Possessions and Hurry out of Egypt

that he had not allowed them to go. "Who will do our hard work for us now?" he asked the soldiers. "Come, let us go after them." Chariots were brought, horses and camels were harnessed, and away rushed the king's soldiers after the Hebrews.

By this time the Hebrews had reached the shores of the Red Sea. They were out of Egypt, and they felt very thankful. But when the Hebrews saw the Egyptians, they were frightened. They rushed to Moses and said, "Why did you bring us out of Egypt? It was better for us to work hard there, and live, than for us to die, here."

"Fear ye not," Moses said. "Wait, and see what God will do for you." God had said to Moses, "Go forward," and he believed that God would help him do just that.

Moses stretched his hand out toward the sea. A fierce wind began to blow. The waves of the sea rippled along the shore. As the wind grew stronger, the waves foamed and roared. The waters piled up on each side, and there, just ahead of Moses was a strip of sand right through the sea. It was a path God had made for his people. High walls of water were on

Moses Stretches Out His Hand

each side, but Moses and his people crossed safely to the other shore.

Singing in Thanksgiving to God

The Egyptians came after the Hebrews. When they saw the narrow strip of sand through the water, they tried to cross on it, just as the Hebrews had done. But the heavy chariots sank into the sand, the chariot wheels came off, and the drivers tumbled over one another. Then the wind stopped blowing, and the waters rolled back over the strip of sand. The terrified Egyptians could not get back to the shore. They were drowned—horses, men in chariots, and the king's soldiers.

But the Hebrews were safe on the opposite shore. They were on their way to the land God had promised them. Falling to their knees, they sang a song of thanksgiving to God. Once again, God had delivered His people from slavery.

Comprehension Exercise

Complete the sentences using the words below.

Red Sea
Moses
blood
Miriam

1. The name

   _____ means "drawn out."

2. Moses had a sister named

   _____ .

3. The Hebrews were saved from death as they put the

   _____ of a lamb on their doors.

4. God destroyed the army of Egypt

   in the _____ .

14 How Jericho's Walls Fell

JOSHUA 4:10—6:27

The day came at last when the Hebrew people reached the end of their long journey across the wilderness. The next morning, they were going to cross the river Jordan into the country which God had promised to give them. Moses, their good friend and leader, was not going with them. He had told the Hebrew people that he was going to leave them. He had said that Joshua would lead them across the Jordan River and help them settle in the beautiful land just beyond it. Then Moses went up into a high mountain and looked across at the country which God had promised to the Hebrews. He would never come back down the mountain, for it was his time to die.

Joshua, a soldier, was now the leader of the Hebrew people. The Hebrews needed a soldier leader. They had much fighting to do before they could take possession of the promised land.

Right across the river from their camp was a city with many fine houses. All around it was a great stone wall. The name of this city was Jericho. The people of Jericho were not friendly toward the Hebrews. They had shut and barred all the great gates of their city, and would not even let any of the people who lived there go in or out of them. They did not want to take any chance of letting the Hebrews in.

But God told Joshua that Jericho was to belong to the Hebrew people.

Jericho, Across the River Jordon

He told him just how to win the city. And Joshua was determined to follow God's plan exactly and get into Jericho.

Early in the morning the Hebrew people crossed the Jordan River. God made for them a dry path across the river, just as He had made a dry path across the Red Sea for them forty years before. First the priests went to the other side, then the soldiers and the strong men, and last of all came the mothers and the little children.

Not a sound did they make, for Joshua had told them that they must keep very still. Soon they were all safely across the river. Tents were unfolded just outside the walls of Jericho, camp fires were built, and the cattle fed. Still no one made a sound.

Seven priests, each carrying a trumpet made of a ram's horn, walked slowly around the walls of Jericho. In front of them and behind them marched the soldiers, carrying their weapons. The next day they did the same thing, and so they did every day for six days. And as they walked around the walls of the city, the seven priests blew their trumpets.

Imagine the noise, with seven men blowing trumpets! The people of Jericho must have thought there was

The Priests Blowing Their Trumpets

a tremendous army just outside their city. Everywhere, they heard the sound of trumpets and of marching feet.

The people in the tents kept still for six long days and nights. Joshua had said that no one but the priests should make a sound until he told them all to shout. And when he told them to shout, they must all shout together.

On the seventh day it was not enough to go around the city just once. On that day the priests, the soldiers, and all the people, too, marched around the walls of Jericho seven times. At the end of the seventh time the priests stopped. The soldiers and the people stood still.

Then the priests blew a long blast on their trumpets. Before they had finished, Joshua called to all the people: "Shout; for the Lord hath given you the city!"

How they shouted! After six long days of quiet, the noise must have seemed louder than a great peal of thunder.

Then a strange thing happened. Those strong stone walls shook and shivered as though something had struck them. Stones began to fall. Then great pieces of the wall fell. And then the great walls themselves tumbled to the ground.

All the Hebrews had to do now to get into Jericho was to walk straight before them into the city. They had won their first victory in the promised land. The city of Jericho was now theirs.

Comprehension Exercise

Complete the sentences using the words below.

Jordan
Joshua
priests
Jericho

1. Moses told the Hebrew people that

   _____ would be their new leader.

2. The Hebrew people crossed the

   _____ river

   to reach the promised land.

3. Joshua lead the Hebrew people against the city of

   _____.

4. The _____ blew the trumpets during the battle of Jericho.

15 Gideon, The New Leader

JUDGES 6:1—8:33

The Midianites were making trouble for the Hebrews. These Midianites, who were a tribe of Arabs, never wanted to live anywhere but in tents. They loved to ride across the desert on swift horses or camels. They did not stay long enough in one place to raise wheat and cattle for food or sheep for wool. So they would steal these things from their neighbors who lived in houses and raised wheat and cattle and sheep. That was why these fierce Arabs came into the Hebrew country.

When the Hebrews' wheat grew tall and was ready to be harvested, the Midianites stole it. When the wool on their sheep grew long and woolly and ready to be cut, the Midianites stole the sheep. Then the Hebrews had no wheat with which to make bread and no wool from which to make warm clothing.

At last the Midianites pitched their goatskin tents all over the beautiful plain that had been covered with the Hebrews' wheat fields, fruit trees, and fine fat cattle. They used the wheat fields to feed their own camels and lean cattle. They stole the Hebrews' goats and sheep from them, so that they could have more skins for their tents and warm wool for their clothes. No wonder the poor Hebrews were so afraid of them that they left their houses and hid in caves among the hills. There they lived in a miserable way–cold, hungry, and homeless.

The Hebrews needed a leader to drive out these Arab robbers. Now this was many years after Joshua's death, and there was no one at the head of the Hebrew people. So God

Midianites Driving Away the Sheep

chose a young man named Gideon, who had faith in Him and who was strong and brave, to be the leader of the Hebrews and to drive out the Midianites.

Gideon had not run away and hidden in a cave. He had stayed in his father's house and threshed some of the wheat he had reaped in spite of the Midianite robbers. Then he hid the wheat from them. And an angel of God appeared before Gideon and said to him, "The Lord is with thee, thou mighty man of valor." Then the angel told Gideon that because he was brave and strong, God had chosen him to go and drive away the wicked Midianites who were making the Hebrew people so unhappy.

Gideon asked the angel how it could be that he was the one to save Israel, as the Hebrew nation was called. "Behold, my family is poor," Gideon said, "and I am the least in my father's house."

Nevertheless, God told Gideon that He would help him, but that first Gideon must do something to show his faith in Him. Gideon's father and the rest of his family did not worship God. They worshipped an image, just as the Hebrew people, when they were in the wilderness, had worshipped the golden calf which Aaron had made for them. God told

Gideon that he must tear down the image, or idol, which his father and his father's friends worshipped. Then he must build an altar unto the true God of the Hebrews, Jehovah.

So Gideon took ten men and tore down the idol which his father had put up. But because he was afraid of his father's anger, and of the anger of the others who worshipped the idol, he did not dare do this in the daytime. So he tore down the idol at night.

In the morning, when the people went to worship their idol, they found that it was destroyed, and in its place there was an altar to Jehovah, the true God.

The people asked one another who had done this. Someone said that Gideon had done it. Then the people went to Gideon's father, and they said to him, "Bring out thy son, that he may die." And they told the father what Gideon had done. But Gideon's father said, "If the god to whom the idol was made is so mighty, he can take care of himself. And if the one who tore down his altar should be punished, let the god do it." So the people did not kill Gideon.

Gideon felt sure that he would make a good leader to drive out the Midianites, but he wanted God to give him a sign. He asked God to show him clearly that he was surely the one chosen to save the Hebrew people from their cruel robber neighbors. Then Gideon did a very strange thing. He had a beautiful fleece–a soft, white woolly sheepskin. Gideon brought out this soft, lovely fleece and spread it out on the ground.

Then he said, "If in the morning there is dew on the fleece and all the ground around it is dry, with not a single drop of dew on it, then I shall know that God has called me to go and drive out the Midianites." In the morning Gideon went out early and looked at the fleece. And it was so full of dew that when he rubbed it together he wrung out of it a bowlful of water. But the ground about the fleece was dry.

Then Gideon said unto God, "Be patient with me, and show me once more with the fleece that I am chosen to drive out the Midianites. Let it now be dry only upon the fleece, and upon all the ground let there be dew."

And that was the way it happened. For the next morning "it was dry upon the fleece only, and there was dew on all the ground."

Gideon Praying for a Sign

Gideon did not hesitate any longer. He was very sure now that God wanted him to drive out the Midianites. Then the Hebrew people would dare to come out of their caves and again live happily in their tents and houses, caring for their fields and cattle, and worshipping the true God.

Brave as he was, Gideon could not drive out the Midianites alone. He must have soldiers. So he sent messengers all over the country, calling for men to help him. Thousands of Hebrew men left their caves and other hiding places to come and follow Gideon. Down the steep mountain sides, over the plains, and along the riverside they came. Then God told Gideon that he did not need so many men. For if a great army drove out the Midianites, the people would think that they had done it by themselves instead of with God's help.

But how was Gideon to know which men to keep? The first thing he did was to send back home every man who was afraid. More than half went home! But God told Gideon that he still had too many men. Now Gideon was both wise and brave. He knew that his soldiers must be brave men. He also wanted men who were chosen by God to drive out the Midianites, just as he himself had been chosen.

God told Gideon what to do. "Bring them down unto the water," He said, "and I will try them for thee there." So Gideon asked all the men to come down with him to a brook. Here he would choose the soldiers who would stand by him until the Midianites were driven out.

Ten thousand men went down to the brook. "Drink," said Gideon. And the men drank. Some dropped down upon their knees, put their faces in the brook, and sucked up the water with their lips. But three hundred of the men dipped up the water with their hands and lapped the water

from them. These were the three hundred whom God told Gideon to take for his soldiers. Perhaps God chose these men because drinking the water from their hands was a more skillful way of drinking than to kneel down and drink from the brook. And Gideon would need skillful men for his followers. "By the three hundred men that lapped will I save you, and deliver the Midianites into thine hand," God told Gideon.

Now Gideon was ready to drive away the Midianites. He peered over the cliffs and looked into the valley below, where the great Arab camp was. There were many more men

Gideon Choosing Soldiers at the Brook

there than the three hundred soldiers Gideon had. But God had told Gideon how to use those three hundred men to save his people.

It was a dark, cloudy night, with no moon and few stars. Gideon and his servant, Phurah, went softly down the mountain side to look at the great Arab camp. In the light of the camp fires Gideon could see the watchmen on guard about the camp. They were telling one another stories. Gideon and Phurah lay quietly in the shadow of the rocks and listened. One Arab soldier was telling some others a strange dream he had. He had seen a cake of barley bread fall into the Arab camp and break down a tent. "This is nothing else save the sword of Gideon," one of the Arabs exclaimed. "He will destroy our army!"

Gideon and Phurah went back to the little Hebrew army on the mountain side. Gideon had learned that the Arabs were afraid of him, and he knew that people who are afraid are easily beaten.

He called out his three hundred soldiers and divided them into three companies of one hundred men each. He told them to carry in one hand a pitcher with a torch burning inside, and that in the other hand every man was to hold a trumpet.

"The sword of the Lord and of Gideon"

These trumpets could make a great noise. When they were blown, there among the hills, it would sound as if there were many times three hundred trumpets.

The soldiers crept quietly down the mountain side with Gideon. One company went to one side of the Arab camp, the second company went to another side, and the third company to still another part of the camp. Then the three hundred Hebrew soldiers stretched themselves out in a single line, making a circle around the big Arab camp. Not a light could be seen or a sound heard. The torches were all hidden in the pitchers, and the trumpets were still. It was late at night. The

Arabs were asleep. Suddenly, all around them, lights flashed out in the dark night as Gideon's three hundred men smashed their pitchers. The startled Arabs must have thought that their whole camp was breaking to pieces. Then three hundred trumpets blared out, and Gideon and his men shouted, "The sword of the Lord and of Gideon!"

"Let us run away before we are all killed by these Hebrews," the frightened Arabs shouted. And run they did. Cattle and camels, sheep and goats were left behind as the Arabs hurried away.

Out from their caves, where they had been hiding, came the Hebrews. They followed close after Gideon and his three hundred men, as they chased the frightened Arabs across the plain and beyond the river to the desert.

Gideon had saved his people through the power of God.

Comprehension Exercise

Complete the sentences using the words below.

God
Phurah
tents
Gideon

1. The Midianites only wanted to live in

   _____.

2. _____

   became the leader of the Hebrews after Joshua died.

3. Gideon and

   _____ went to spy on the Arab camp.

4. Gideon saved the people of Israel through the power of

   _____.

16 The Hebrews' First King

1 SAMUEL 8:1—10:27

All the countries near Israel, the land of the Hebrews, had kings to rule over them. Now the Hebrews wanted a king just like the ungodly nations.

These people of Israel, as the Hebrews were called, were growing rich. And the richer they grew the more trouble they had. The people from the other countries tried to take away from them their land and their cattle. A king would fight their battles for them, the Hebrews thought. Then, while the king and his soldiers were driving away the robbers, the people could stay at home to care for their cattle and their fruitful fields.

One Hebrew did not want a king. He was Samuel, an old man who for many years had been the Judge of Israel. Samuel believed that trusting in God was better than trusting in a king.

Samuel prayed to God for help. God told him that he should listen to the people and choose a king for them. Then Samuel asked God to help him choose a man who would be a good king and who would rule wisely over Israel. And in answer to his prayer, Saul came.

Saul was a handsome young man, tall and strong. He was out looking for his father's asses, which were lost, when he met Samuel. Samuel had been told by God to watch for Saul. He kept Saul with him all night, and the next morning walked

The Anointing of Saul

down with him to the city gate. There he told Saul to stand still. He poured the anointing oil upon his head, which meant that God had chosen Saul for a special purpose. Then Samuel kissed him, and called him king.

Now Samuel made a great feast for all the Hebrews, to tell them about their new king, and show him to them. Saul was there with his family and all his relatives. Once more Samuel told the Hebrew people that they were making a great mistake in having a king. Some day, he said, they would be sorry, and wish that they had trusted in God alone. But the people would not listen. They looked at Saul, who was "higher than any of the people from his shoulders and upward." How proud they were to have this grand looking man for their king! Surely he would fight their battles for them and drive away the wicked neighbors who were always tormenting and robbing them. The Hebrews came forward and greeted their new king. "God save the king!" they shouted.

Saul was a great fighter. He led the Hebrews out to battle, and drove away many of their bad neighbors. He grew powerful, and the people of the countries near by became afraid of him. But Saul was making a great mistake. He was trusting in his own strength alone, instead of having faith in God. He could fight battles, but he was not wise enough to rule his kingdom well. Poor King Saul!

His kingdom was not a joy to him but a burden, because he did not know how to take care of it. And he would not go to God for help, or take advice from Samuel, the wise old prophet who had made him king. Samuel loved Saul, and was bitterly disappointed that this first Hebrew king should forget God and think only of having his own way. King Saul did not have peace and joy in his life because he tried to fight God's enemies in his own strength.

Comprehension Exercise

Complete the sentences using the words below.

strength
save
Saul
Samuel

1. The first King in Israel was named

   _____.

2. The prophet

   _____

   anointed the new king.

3. The Hebrews greeted their new king by saying, "God

   _____ the king!"

4. Saul trusted in his own

   _____ to be a good king.

17 The Anointing of David

1 SAMUEL 16:1—23

Samuel saw that King Saul was not a good ruler for Israel. Saul had been a good soldier, but that was all. Samuel prayed to God for help in choosing a new king. And God said to him, "How long wilt thou mourn for Saul, seeing I have rejected him from reigning over Israel? Fill thine horn with oil, and go, I will send thee to Jesse the Bethlehemite: for I have provided me a king among his sons."

At first Samuel was afraid to go. If Saul should hear that he had gone to Bethlehem to choose a new king, he would surely kill him. But God had told Samuel to go. Besides, he was growing older and feebler every day, and every day Saul was becoming a worse king.

It was the time of the Hebrews' yearly feast. Samuel decided to go to Bethlehem and celebrate the feast with the people there. No one would suspect his real errand. While the people were gathered at the feast, Samuel could see all of Jesse's sons and choose one of them for a king. Samuel was going to anoint this young man with oil, just as he had anointed Saul. This would show that the chosen one was set aside for some special purpose, but it would not show anyone that he would some day become king of Israel.

So Samuel went to Bethlehem, and at the feast he saw Jesse and his sons. The oldest son was a fine-looking young man. For a moment Samuel thought surely he was the one who should be the future king of Israel. But God said to Samuel: "Look not on his countenance, or on the height of his stature; because I have refused him: for the Lord seeth

Samuel and Jesse

not as man seeth; for man looketh on the outward appearance, but the Lord looketh on the heart."

Two more sons passed before Samuel–big, fine fellows, fearless soldiers in Saul's army. But Samuel felt that God had not chosen either of them. At last Samuel had seen all the seven sons who were with Jesse. But he did not feel that God wanted any one of them for Israel's next king.

"Are here all thy children?" Samuel asked Jesse. And Jesse answered, "There remaineth yet the youngest, and, behold, he keepeth the sheep." In those days this was much the same as saying, "He does not amount to much; it is foolish to ask to see him." But Samuel said to Jesse, "Send and fetch him: for we will not sit down till he come hither."

David, the shepherd lad, came in, his cheeks rosy and his face pleasant. And Samuel took the horn of anointing oil and poured it on David's head. For God had said to Samuel, "Arise, anoint him: for this is he."

David knew that he had been set apart for something, but he did not know what it was, for Samuel did not tell him. Samuel thought it was better to let David prove that he would make a good king by the things that he did and the way he did

Samuel Anoints David

them. He liked the pleasant face and kindly ways of this young shepherd lad, but he was going to make David show his worth. And so Samuel left David and returned to his home.

Not long after this, David went to live for a time with King Saul. It happened this way. King Saul had dreadful spells of being gloomy and unhappy. When these spells came over him, he was so miserable that he would not eat or sleep or speak to anyone. King Saul's servants were very much worried about the king. They wanted to do something to help him. They knew that he dearly loved music. If they could find someone who could play the harp well, and sing, they thought that it might help cure the king.

One of King Saul's servants knew Jesse's family, and remembered that one of Jesse's sons, David, could play the harp. So this servant asked the king for his permission to send for "a cunning player on an harp that he shall play with his hand, and thou shalt be well." And Saul said, "Provide me now a man that can play well, and bring him to me." So a messenger was sent from the king's house to Jesse with King Saul's command to send David to

David, the Shepherd Lad

him. Jesse went out to the field where David was taking care of the sheep.

How surprised David must have been to learn that he was wanted in the king's house! He set out for the city of the king with his harp and songs. David also brought an ass laden with gifts for the king from his father, Jesse.

In the king's house David's cheerful face and kindly words pleased everyone. Even the gloomy king loved this ruddy shepherd lad so much that he took him for his armor bearer, and sent a message to Jesse asking that David be allowed to stay with him.

So David stayed in the king's house. His fingers moved lightly over the harp strings, and his songs brought cheer to all the household. When Saul was taken with one of his terrible spells, David would play to him. The music would quiet the king at once. He would grow calmer and listen with interest as the shepherd boy sang to the music of the harp.

David's songs must have been happy songs, filled with thoughts of the sunshine and the stars, the grassy hillsides and the singing birds, the cooling breezes and the peaceful fields he knew so well. These songs did King Saul so much good that he

A City in the Hebrews' Country

almost felt that he was well again. He wanted David always to be near him. But David the shepherd lad, living in the city with the king, was the same David he had always been. He was gentle in manner, and brave and fearless too, for God was with David, and David trusted in Him.

18 David and Goliath

1 SAMUEL 17:1—54

Now the Philistine enemies came into the Hebrew country with their armies to make war on the people of Israel. They made their camp on a mountain side near a valley. On the opposite side of the valley there was another mountain, and there the armies of King Saul made their camp.

David's three oldest brothers were in King Saul's army, but David had gone back to Bethlehem to take care of his father's sheep. One morning Jesse, David's father, told David to leave the sheep with a servant and go to the king's camp to take some bread and corn to his brothers. Jesse wanted to hear how his sons were getting along, whether they were well, and whether they were having plenty to eat. Besides sending food to his sons, Jesse gave David some cheeses to give to the captain who was in command over the brothers.

David was very glad to have a chance to go to the army camp. When he arrived, the Hebrew sol-diers were ready for battle. It looked as if they were going to fight with their Philistine enemies right away.

Across the valley the Philistines were in battle formation, too. David found his brothers, and gave them the food which their father had sent them.

While the brothers stood talking together, a giant came out in front of the Philistine army. His name was Goliath, and he was the champion of the Philistines. He wore a suit of armor, so that no spears or swords could hurt him. On his head he wore a brass helmet, and in his hand he carried a heavy spear. Before him went a man carrying the giant's great shield.

Goliath stood out in front of the Philistine army and shouted to the Hebrew soldiers. He taunted them, and asked them why they were getting ready for battle. "Send a man down here to fight with me," he said. "If he kills me, the Philistines will be your servants; but if I kill him, then you must be the servants of the Philistines."

When the Hebrews heard Goliath, they were terribly afraid. The soldiers ran back so that they would be farther away from him.

David was very much angered by this boastful giant. "Who is this uncircumcised Philistine, that he should defy the armies of the living God?" he asked. And he said that he thought it was shameful to let Goliath taunt them so. This made David's oldest brother angry at him. To think that this young shepherd boy should question the courage of the Hebrew soldiers! Who wouldn't be afraid of Goliath? And he asked David why he had left his sheep and come down to the camp. "You have only come down to see the battle," he scolded David.

"What have I now done?" David asked his brother. And he turned away from him and started to talk to another man in the same fearless way about Goliath. David learned that King Saul, too, was afraid of Goliath, and that he would do great things for any man who should kill this giant. The king would make him very rich and would give him his daughter in marriage. David kept asking the soldiers why they all were afraid of this giant.

At last David's words came to King Saul's ears. At once the king sent for David and asked him what it was that he was saying. David told Saul what he had said. Then he offered to go himself and fight Goliath. Saul was greatly surprised at David's courage, and he said to him, "Thou art not able to go against this Philis-

tine to fight with him: for thou art but a youth, and he is a man of war." David told Saul that he had done some fighting when he had been keeping his father's sheep.

Once, he said, a lion had come to take a lamb out of the flock. David had gone after the lion and had killed him. And another time, when a bear had tried to kill one of his lambs, David had fought and killed the bear, too.

"God saved me from the lion and the bear David told King Saul, and He will deliver me out of the hand of this Philistine."

Then Saul said to David, "Go, and the Lord be with thee."

And he gave David his own armor, and put a brass helmet on his head, and gave him a sword. He thought that David would surely need the very best weapons and armor to fight Goliath.

But David was not yet a soldier. "I cannot go with these," he said, and he took them off. He took his shepherd's staff in his hand, and went down to the brook which ran through the valley.

There he chose five smooth stones and put them into a shepherd's bag which he had with him. Then, with

David with His Sling

his sling in his hand, David went out in front of the Hebrew army, to defy Goliath.

When Goliath saw that one of the Hebrews was coming to fight him, he came a few steps nearer. The man who carried his shield went before him.

But when the giant saw that the one who defied him was only a youth, he was full of scorn for David, and taunted him. And the men of the Philistine army laughed to see the shepherd boy, with only his little sling for a weapon, come out to challenge the mighty giant who was their champion.

But David stood before Goliath and answered him bravely:

"Thou comest to me with a sword, and with a spear, and with a shield: but I come to thee in the name of the Lord of hosts, the God of the armies of Israel, whom thou hast defied."

David told Goliath that he was sure God would help him win the victory, and that it would be God's victory, not his.

Then Goliath went forward to meet David. And David ran toward Goliath. "And David put his hand in his bag, and took out a stone, and slang it, and smote the Philistine in his forehead, that the stone sunk into his forehead; and he fell upon his face to the earth." So David killed the giant with a sling and a stone. He then ran up to the evil Goliath and cut off his head.

When the Philistines saw that Goliath was dead, they ran, and the men of Israel ran after them.

And Saul called for David, and praised him. He told David that he must not go home again, but must stay with the king. So once more David went to live with King Saul. "And David went out whithersoever Saul sent him, and behaved himself wisely."

David's victory was known and remembered by all. Goliath's sword was given into the care of a priest to keep in memory of that day. But later, when David badly needed a sword, the priest gave the giant's sword to him. "There is none like that," David said, as he took the great weapon.

Comprehension Exercise

Complete the sentences using the words below.

Goliath
David
harp
Jesse

1. After God rejected King Saul, He told Samuel to anoint

   _____ as the next king in Israel.

2. David had a father named

   _____.

3. When David was a shepherd he learned to play the

   _____ and sing.

4. David killed the giant

   _____ with the help of Almighty God.

19 David and Jonathan

1 SAMUEL 18:1—19:42, 22:6—8, AND 23:14—24:22

The prince, Jonathan, was with King Saul when he called for David, after the death of Goliath. Jonathan looked on with interest as David told the king about the victory which God had given him over the giant. He liked the simple, modest way in which David told of his great deed. He liked his frank, pleasant face and his kind eyes. The more he looked at the shepherd boy, the better he liked him. "He has a strong spirit, brave and true," Jonathan thought. "God must be with him."

In those days, people showed respect and love for a friend by taking off their outer garment and giving it to this friend. Jonathan took off his robe and put it on David. Then he gave David his sword, his bow, and his girdle. Now David was only a shepherd, while Jonathan was a prince, the son of a king. So this was Jonathan's way of saying, "You are as much of a prince at heart as I am, and I want you for my friend."

From that day Jonathan and David were close friends.

King Saul was not like his son Jonathan. The gloomy king soon grew jealous of David, and began to hate him. Saul could see that God was with David, and he knew that God was no longer with him. Besides, Saul was terribly afraid of losing his kingdom; Samuel had told him that he would lose it. The braver David was and the more the people loved him, the more Saul thought that the next king might be David.

David had become a great soldier. At first he had not known much about the ways of a soldier, and certainly he had not looked like one. But deep in David's heart was a spirit that could never be beaten. Saul and his men soon discovered that David could win battles and drive away the enemy better than many older soldiers.

One time David won a great victory. On his way home some women danced about the victorious army and sang to them. In their song they said, "Saul hath slain his thousands, and David his ten thousands." This made Saul very angry.

"They say ten thousands for David and only thousands for me," he grumbled. "What can he have more but the kingdom?" And King Saul

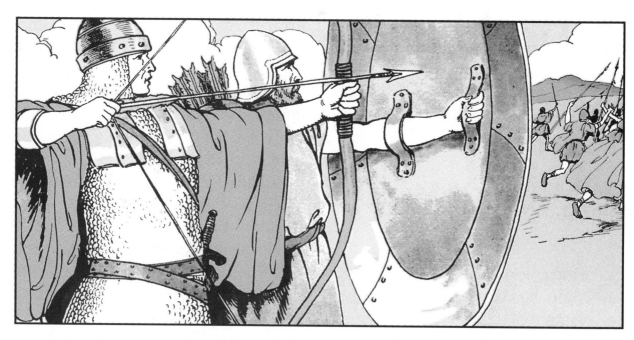

The Philistines Flee from King Saul's Soldiers

was so jealous of David that he wanted to kill him to get rid of him.

The day after the women had sung the song about David's ten thousands, Saul had another of his dreadful spells. Again David sang and played for him. But this time his music did not help Saul, because the king's heart was filled with rage and jealousy. He rose up from his chair, grasped his spear, and threw it at David. It missed David and struck the wall. Saul threw it again, and once more David barely escaped.

Then Saul tried to kill David another way. He encouraged him to go into battles against the Philistines. Saul thought that in one of these battles David would surely be killed by a Phi-listine. But David did not die in battle. God kept him safe.

King Saul Hurls His Spear at David

It made Jonathan very sad to see how his father hated David. Jonathan was not jealous of David, even when he thought that David might be king instead of himself.

"Why do you wish to hurt David?" Jonathan asked his father. "He has done some very good things for you. You saw him deliver Israel from the giant and the Philistines, and you were glad."

For a little while Saul was ashamed of himself. He promised Jonathan that he would not hurt David. Then David won another battle over the Philistines. He came home unhurt and with the people singing his praises. This made the king savage. "David must die, or I shall surely lose my kingdom," Saul kept thinking to himself all the time.

At last David realized that his life was no longer safe near Saul. He did not dare stay in the king's house any longer. So that night he escaped through a window. In the morning the king sent messengers to David's room to kill him, but David was gone. Saul was very angry. He learned that David had gone to Samuel's home, and he sent messengers to bring him back. But the messengers did not bring back David. So the

King Saul in Battle

king himself started out to find David and to kill him.

When David learned that Saul was on the way to find him, he left Samuel's house and went back to find his friend Jonathan. "What have I done that your father should hate me so?" David asked him. Jonathan could not answer that. But he said to David, "Whatever my father does, I know. And I cannot believe that he has really ordered your death." "As thy soul liveth," David told Jonathan, "there is but a step between me and death." Then Jonathan believed David and he said to him, "Whatever you wish me to do, that shall I do for you." And he and David sat down together and planned what they could do to save David's life from the king.

The next day was a feast day, and the king expected David to be in his place at the dinner table. "I do not dare eat with the king," David told Jonathan. "Let me go and hide myself in the fields for three days. Then we can see how great is the king's anger toward me. When the king asks for me, tell him that I might have gone to visit my family in Bethlehem. If he says that is well, let me know and I will return, but if he is angry I will stay away." And the two friends planned a way for Jonathan to send David word of how the king felt toward him.

Then Jonathan went with David to a rocky field outside the city. There they found a great rock with a cave

David's Place is Empty

behind it, where David could hide until he heard from Jonathan.

The next day–the feast day–when dinner time came David's place was empty. Saul was furious. The next day David's place again was empty. "Where has he gone?" Saul raved. And when Jonathan said that perhaps he had gone to see his family at Bethlehem, Saul did not believe him. He said terrible things to Jonathan. "Why do you make this shepherd lad–this son of a farmer–your friend?" Saul asked him. "Do you not know that so long as David lives and is so popular with the people, you will never be king? Go, get him and bring him here, for he shall surely die."

Jonathan dared to ask his father, "What has David done that he should be put to death?" The furious king answered him by seizing his spear and throwing it at his son. For a whole day Jonathan ate nothing, because he was so grieved about his father and David. Before this, he had still hoped that the king had not meant all he had said about killing David. But now he knew that the king did mean every word of it. He knew that David was not safe in Saul's house, or even in the same country with Saul. Jonathan must warn his friend as he and David had

Jonathan Warning David

planned. Then he would help him to escape from the cruel king.

Now Jonathan was a great archer. Jonathan's bow must have been nearly as tall as himself. It was strong, and with it he was able to send heavy arrows a long distance.

But the next time Jonathan shot them from his bow it would not be to kill; it would be to carry a warning to the waiting David. And so well had David and Jonathan planned just how this should be done, that even if Saul himself had been there watching, he never would have suspected what was going on.

On the third morning after David had talked with Jonathan, he was watching for a message from his friend. He saw Jonathan come into the field with a boy. Jonathan had his great bow and his sharp arrows with him. He sent the boy ahead of him, saying, "Run, find out now the arrows which I shoot." Then Jonathan drew his bow to his shoulder and fitted an arrow to it. He shot the arrow far across the field, toward the rock behind which David was hiding. It looked as if he were shooting at a mark. Again he fitted an arrow to his bow and let it fly. A third time he did this, and an arrow sped across the field. Now three arrows lay near the great rock, and the lad ran to pick them up. Then Jonathan called to him, "Make speed, haste, stay not."

David, watching and listening behind the rock, knew what those words meant. He knew that they had been meant for him instead of for the boy. He knew that he must go far away and hide from the king, or the king would surely kill him.

But Jonathan could not bear to send away his good friend without saying good-by to him. So he gave his bow and arrows to the lad and told him to carry them back home. As soon as the boy was out of sight, he hurried toward the great rock where David was. The two friends kissed each other, and wept. They must part, for David would have to leave his home, and even his country, in order to save his life. David said good-by to his dear friend.

And Jonathan said to David, "Go in peace... the Lord be between me and thee ... forever." Then David fled from that place, and Jonathan returned sadly to his home.

Poor David! No place was safe for him. He escaped to Gath, a neighboring country, but his life was in danger there. Then he went to live in a cave called Adullam.

Soon other men who were hiding from the anger of Saul began to come to the cave to be with David. There were too many men to hide in one cave. So they went to live in the forest of Hareth.

They heard that the city of Keilah was being robbed by the Philistines. So they went down to this city and fought with the Philistines. They drove them away and saved the people of Keilah. When Saul heard of that, he started to send his soldiers to Keilah to take David prisoner. But David learned of King Saul's plan and went into the wilderness with his men—there were about six hundred

of them now—and there they lived on a wild mountain.

Saul soon learned where David was hiding. He and his soldiers went after him, but they did not find him. David left the mountain and went into a forest. There David's friend Jonathan found him, and told him again of his love. He promised that he would do all he could to keep the king from finding David. "And thou shalt be king over Israel," Jonathan told David, "and I shall be next unto thee." Then the faithful friend went back to his home, and David returned to the wilderness.

Some people went to Saul and told him that they knew exactly where David could be found. Saul took three thousand men and went to the mountain wilderness where David was hiding.

King Saul Resting in the Cave

Shepherds with Their Sheep

All about this part of the country there were shepherds and their sheep. These shepherds were very friendly with David's men, and let them use their sheepfolds as shelters and hiding places. And in return, David's men protected them and their sheep.

On a hillside where a shepherd had fixed a sheltered place for his sheep, Saul saw a cave. Being tired, he went into it alone to rest for a time. Saul did not imagine that this was the very cave in which David was hiding. With David were a few of his followers. When they saw Saul come into the cave, they whispered to David, "Behold, thine enemy is delivered into thine hand." And they thought that surely David would kill Saul. But David did not. "The Lord forbid that I should do this thing unto my master, the Lord's anointed," he said. But he did creep up behind the king and cut off a piece of his outer robe.

When Saul left the cave and went on his way, David also went out of the cave. He called after Saul, "My lord the king!" And when Saul looked behind him, David bowed himself to the earth. Then David spoke to Saul and asked him why he believed that he, David, would try to hurt him. "You can see," David said to him, "that you were in my power in the cave. My men told me to kill you, but I would not harm you. See, here is a piece of your robe, which I took when I might have killed you. This will show you that I intend no harm against you, yet you hunt me to kill me. Who am I that the king of Israel should come out after me? The Lord ... plead my cause, and deliver me out of thine hand."

When David had stopped speaking, Saul said, "Is this thy voice, my son David?" and he wept. And he said to David, "Thou are more righteous than I: for thou hast rewarded me good, whereas I have rewarded thee evil." Then he thanked David for not killing him when he could have done so. And he told David that he knew that when he became king of Israel the kingdom would prosper under him.

Then Saul took his men and went home. But David and his men stayed in their strongholds in the mountains. It still was not safe for David to return to the king's house.

Now the Philistines gathered together their armies to march into the Hebrew country. The Philistines had feared David, but they were no longer afraid of Saul. So into Israel they marched, with long lines of men with glittering spears, archers with their great bows, prancing horses and heavy chariots.

Saul's heart was sick with fear. He looked at his own miserable army and he knew that his men could do little against the thousands of Philistine soldiers encamped in the valley. Samuel was dead now, and David was not there. Saul felt that he no longer had anyone to help him.

It happened just as Saul had feared. In the battle the frightened men of Israel ran away in every direction. Arrows whizzed through the air, swords flashed, and chariots rumbled over the battlefield. Jonathan was slain. Two of Jonathan's brothers

Hebrew Soldiers Running from the Philistines

were killed also. King Saul was badly wounded by the Philistine archers, and for fear that he might be taken prisoner by the enemy, he took his sword and fell upon it.

A soldier who had escaped from the battle came to David and told him about it, and of the death of Saul and Jonathan. David was very sad, and so were the men who were with him. "And they mourned, and wept, and fasted until evening, for Saul, and for Jonathan his son, and for the people of the Lord, and for the house of Israel; because they were fallen by the sword."

David made a song to tell about the love he had for Jonathan. And later, in memory of his friend the great archer, he made it a rule that the children of his kingdom should be taught the use of the bow.

Comprehension Exercise

Complete the sentences using the words below.

Saul
Jonathan
David
archer

1. The prince in Israel under King Saul was named

   _____.

2. King Saul became very angry and jealous with

   _____.

3. Jonathan was a great

   _____.

4. David had a chance to kill

   King _____ in a cave.

20 King David

**2 SAMUEL 1:1—12
AND 2:1—5:5**

King Saul was dead. No longer could he trouble David or drive him and his followers from their homes. Now David could leave his hiding places in the wilderness and return home. First he went to Judah, which was the part of Israel where his relatives lived. He took the men who had been with him in the wilderness, and their families to Judah.

The men of Judah came to David, and made him their king.

David did not try to make himself king of all Israel, for Saul's son, Ishbosheth, had been called king of Israel. Abner, the captain of Saul's army who had eaten at the same table with David when David had lived in King Saul's house, had made Ishbosheth king. David did not care, for he knew that God would show him when it was time for him to become king of Israel.

But Joab, the captain of David's army, and Abner, Saul's old captain and now Ishbosheth's captain, were determined to quarrel and fight with each other. Joab thought that David ought to be king over the whole of Israel, while Abner thought that Saul's son should be king over all Israel, including Judah, where David was now king. So David's brave men and Saul's old soldiers kept fighting each other. David's men won nearly every battle, so that in this long war David grew stronger and stronger and Saul's son, Ishbosheth, grew weaker and weaker.

Then Ishbosheth made his good captain Abner very angry. Instead of thanking Abner for helping him to be king, Ishbosheth found fault with him. Abner decided that he had done wrong to stand by Saul's son. He decided that, after all, David was the right one to be king over Israel,

David, King of Judah

even though he was not a king's son. So Abner told Ishbosheth that he was going to go over to David's side, to help David become king of all Israel. And Ishbosheth did not answer Abner a word, because he was afraid of him.

Then Abner sent messengers to David, offering to help him become Israel's king.

David sent word to this brave soldier that he would be glad to have him on his side. Then Abner talked to the elders of Israel, telling them that God already had said that David should be the one to save Israel from the Philistines. And he told others the same, and asked for their help in making David the next king of Israel. After this, Abner took twenty of his men and went to join David in the land of Judah. David made a great feast for this brave army leader and for his men. But Abner did not stay quietly in Judah with David.

He started out to see other important people in Israel about making David king.

Joab had been away when Abner and his twenty men had come to David. When Joab returned, he was very angry to hear that Abner had been there. "He came to deceive thee." Joab told David, "and to

The Journey to Jerusalem

know thy going out and thy coming in, and to know all that thou doest."

Then, without David's knowledge, Joab went after Abner and killed him. This made David very angry. He commanded Joab to mourn for Abner, and David himself wept, and mourned for Abner. Thankfully, the people understood that it was Joab, who had caused Abner's death, and that David was not in any way to blame for it.

When Ishbosheth heard of Abner's death, he felt very weak. No strong man now was left to take his part. And indeed he had needed Abner, for soon afterward some wicked man killed him in his bed as he slept. Messengers ran to David with the news. David was sad to think that this wicked deed had been done, and that Saul's son had been killed in such a cowardly way.

Israel was now without a king. So the chief people and elders of this Hebrew country came to David. They reminded him of the battles he had won for Israel while Saul was king, and that God had told him that some day he should be "a captain over Israel." So they asked David to become their leader, and the elders anointed him king of Israel.

Three times David had been anointed: first by Samuel, then by the men of Judah, and now by the elders of Israel. Surely he must have deserved his kingdom. David was well thought of by everyone–"whatsoever the king did pleased all the people."

David was now thirty years old. He had been ruling over Judah for seven years; now he and all his men moved to Jerusalem, where David established a great city. From there he ruled the kingdom of Israel wisely and well. He drove out the Philistines who dared to come into Israel, seeking to kill the new king. He conquered other enemies of the Hebrew people–the Moabites and the Syrians–and he made the Moabites his servants.

King David grew great, and the Lord was with him.

Comprehension Exercise

Complete the sentences using the words below.

Abner
Joab
Judah
Jerusalem

1. After Saul died, David became king of

   _____.

2. The mighty captain

   _____ left King Ishbosheth to help David become the king of Israel.

3. _____ killed Abner without telling David.

4. King David established the great city of

   _____ as he ruled the kingdom of Israel.

Stories From The New Testament

21 The Story of the Shepherds

MATTHEW 1:18—25 AND LUKE 2:1—39

Long, long ago, on a far away hillside, some shepherds were keeping watch over their sheep by night. Suddenly one of the shepherds was sure that he heard music. He looked up at the stars and saw them sparkling as though they were alive. He called to his companions to watch them. And when the shepherds looked up, they saw in the sky just above them something very wonderful.

There in the sky, very near to them, was a shining angel. All about him was such a wonderful light that it made everything on the hillside glow.

At first the astonished shepherds were frightened. But the angel spoke to them so kindly that they soon were at peace.

"Fear not," the heavenly messenger said, "for, behold, I bring you good tidings of great joy." Then the watching shepherds gathered together to hear the angel speak.

"Tonight," the angel told them, "is the most wonderful night since the world was made. It is a night for which the Hebrew people have waited very long. For this day there is born in Bethlehem a Savior who is Christ the Lord." And the angel told the shepherds where to find the baby Christ.

Then the music grew louder and clearer. It was a song, and a great company of angels was singing it. These angels had suddenly appeared in the sky, beside the heavenly messenger. "Glory to God in the highest," they sang, "and on earth peace, good will toward men."

After the light had faded and the song had ended, the shepherds did not wait a moment. They hurried to Bethlehem to find the new-born Lord that the angel had told them of. They wanted to worship Him at once.

When they reached the little town of Bethlehem, the shepherds went straight to the inn where the angel had said they were to find the little Christ Child.

GLORY TO GOD IN THE HIGHEST, AND ON EARTH PEACE, GOOD WILL TOWARD MEN.

Luke 2:14

The large, dimly lighted courtyard of the inn was crowded with people. Tired travelers were sleeping on the stone floor. Sleepy donkeys and camels nodded and blinked at the shepherds.

How could the searching shepherds hope to find a tiny baby in the midst of such a crowd? But the angel had told them that the little Christ Child was here. They found Him, lying on some straw in a manger, with his mother Mary, for there had not been room inside the inn for them.

The shepherds stood very still as they looked down upon the tiny baby. Perhaps they were thinking again of the angel's message. Then, one by one, they tiptoed quietly out of the courtyard. They told others about the wonderful message which had come to them on the hillside, and about the baby Christ whom they had just seen. "And all they that heard it wondered at those things which were told them by the shepherds."

As these humble shepherds went slowly back to the green hillside, where their sheep were sleeping, their hearts were filled with joy. And perhaps they sang the song they had heard the angels sing: "Glory to God in the highest, and on earth peace, good will toward men."

The Crowded Courtyard of the Inn

22 The Magi and the Star

MATTHEW 2:1—23

Some Wise Men in the East, who were called the Magi, spent every night watching the stars. Their big books, or scrolls, had told them that an important new star, very bright and beautiful, would soon appear in the sky. While this star was in the sky, the books said, a new and greater King would be born in the Hebrew country. The Magi planned to go to Jerusalem to worship this King when the star appeared.

At last the Magi saw the new star in the sky, and they started on their long journey to Jerusalem. How far they traveled and how long it took them to reach that distant city no one knows. They must have been weary men when their tired camels passed through the gates of the city of Jerusalem. But they went on to the palace of King Herod, who was the ruler of Palestine under the power of Rome.

"We have seen in the East a wonderful star," they told Herod, "the star which brings good news of a child born to be the King of the Jews. Tell us where we can find this King, so we may honor Him."

Herod was troubled. He did not want to hear of any other king in his country but himself. Had these strangers from the East learned from the stars something that he did not know?

Herod called the lawyers and the chief priests to his palace. "Tell me," he demanded, "where do our writings say Christ is to be born?" "In Bethlehem of Judea," they answered.

Wicked King Herod was badly frightened. He called the Magi to him secretly and asked them about the star. Then he sent them to Bethle-

Maji Searching the Ancient Scrolls

hem to search for the Child. "And when ye have found Him," Herod told the Wise Men, "bring me word again, that I may come and worship Him also."

Through the gates of Jerusalem and down the rocky road toward Bethlehem the three Magi traveled. There was little welcome from his own people for the Christ Child. But these strangers from the East had journeyed over mountains and deserts and rivers that they might bring their rich gifts to the little new-born King. High in the sky shone the bright star, guiding them here as it had done in the East.

The star still shone above them as they rode through the narrow streets of Bethlehem. Straight above one little house it hung. Into that home the Wise Men went, and there they found the child Jesus and his mother, Mary. As Mary watched, the Magi bowed low before the Child. Then they spread before Him their gifts of gold, rich spices, and sweet-smelling incense.

Now the Wise Men were ready to return to their homes in the East. But they did not go to Jerusalem to tell King Herod about the Child. God warned them in a dream not to go back to Herod. So they returned to their country by another road, a road that did not lead through Jerusalem.

Herod waited and waited, but no Magi came. When he heard that they had gone back to the East another way, he was furious. "I will kill that little new-born King of the Jews if I have to kill all the boy babies in Bethlehem," he shouted. And that is exactly what he tried to do. But he never found the baby Jesus.

Comprehension Exercise

Complete the sentences using the words below.

Herod
Bethlehem
manger
Magi

1. The angel told the shepherds to

   go to _____.

2. The shepherds found the Christ Child lying in a

   _____.

3. The Wise Men from the East were called the

   _____.

4. _____ tried to kill the baby Jesus.

23 The Escape

MATTHEW 2:13—23

After the Wise Men had mounted their camels and had ridden away from the home of the baby Jesus, Joseph and Mary went to sleep. Suddenly Joseph awakened Mary. "We must start at once for Egypt," he told her. "The Child's life is in danger. King Herod is going to try to kill Him." No doubt Mary asked her husband anxiously why he thought so. And Joseph answered, "An angel of the Lord warned me in a dream that we should flee from Herod into Egypt." So Joseph and Mary must have packed the few things they would need and started for Egypt that very night.

Just outside of Bethlehem was an inn, called a *khan*, where many travelers stopped on their way to Egypt. It made a good halting place for people and caravans making a long journey. Here their camels, donkeys, horses, and other animals could be watered and fed. The travelers themselves could also rest. Joseph may have gone to the khan to see about buying a camel or a donkey for the journey to Egypt. He knew they must lose no time in leaving Bethlehem, if they were to save the Child from King Herod.

Hour after hour Joseph and Mary and the baby Jesus hurried over the wilderness on their long journey to Egypt. On and on they went toward safety. When the soldiers of King Herod reached Bethlehem, they would not find the Child they had come to destroy.

It was hot in Egypt, and very uncomfortable, and Joseph and Mary were anxious to go back home. After a time news reached them that Herod had died. Now that the cruel king was gone, they thought the child Jesus would be safe.

At the *khan* near Bethlehem

Another dream came to Joseph in which an angel told him that he might return to Palestine with Mary and the Child. "They are dead which sought the young Child's life," the angel said.

So Joseph and Mary and the baby Jesus traveled back to their own country. How happy Mary and Joseph must have felt, thinking that soon they would be at home again! But they could not go back to Bethlehem, because King Herod's son, a man as wicked as his father, was now ruler over Judea, that part of Palestine where Bethlehem was.

Mary and Joseph had lived in Nazareth, a pretty little town in Galilee, before they had gone to Bethlehem. So Joseph took Mary and her little Son to Nazareth. Here, among their old friends, the family made a new home.

24 In the Temple

LUKE 2:41—52

Every year, at a certain time, people from all over Palestine went to Jerusalem. They went to celebrate the Feast of the Passover in the great temple there, in memory of the time in Egypt when God had spared the children of the Hebrews. It was the custom for every family to sacrifice a lamb on the temple altar. Some people wished to give more than a single lamb, so they brought with them cattle and goats.

This was the reason for the long procession which wound slowly through mountain paths and across grassy meadows toward Jerusalem. Camels and donkeys, chattering children, nicely dressed women, and serious-faced men—all these were in the procession. And there were cattle and lambs, and frisky young goats which would stop often for a nibble of grass or a juicy thistle.

Imagine how crowded the big city of Jerusalem was when these thousands of strangers visited it. In nearly every house there were guests. But even then, there was not enough room inside the walls of Jerusalem to care for all the people who came to the feast. So the people who could not find a place to stay inside the city camped in the valley just outside the city walls.

To someone looking down from the city walls, it must have seemed like a big army encamped around Jerusalem. But all these people had come peacefully to attend the Passover Feast. Some years, it is said, more than two million people journeyed to Jerusalem for the Feast of the Passover.

Camping Outside the Walls of Jerusalem

Among the caravans journeying toward the city gates was one from Nazareth. And in this caravan from Nazareth were Mary and Joseph and the boy Jesus. He was twelve years old, and this was his first visit to Jerusalem. And Mary and Joseph found a stopping place in the city instead of having to camp outside its walls.

Jerusalem must have seemed very wonderful to this twelve-year-old Boy. There were many streets and houses, and fine shops, where many curious things were sold. But there was only one place in all the wonderful city which Jesus wished to visit. He had heard about the great temple where the Passover Feast was kept. He had been told about the wise Hebrew men who studied and taught there. And so He wanted to go to the temple, which He knew was God's house.

During the week of the Passover all the animals which the people had brought with them were sacrificed upon the altar. Now the week was over, and friends who met only once a year at these feasts were saying good-by. Caravan after caravan moved slowly down the rocky hillsides on their homeward way.

Some caravans started late in the afternoon, planning to stop for the night at the first well or spring they reached. But whether a caravan traveled all day, or only two or three hours late in the day, it was called a "day's journey."

At the little town of Beeroth there was a fine spring of water. Perhaps that was where the caravan going back to Nazareth camped. At this over-night stopping place Mary and Joseph missed Jesus. They thought He must be with relatives or friends in some other part of the caravan. From friend to friend they went, hoping to find Him. But He was not in any other part of the caravan. Then Mary and Joseph decided that Jesus must still be in Jerusalem, so back to the city they hurried.

Three long, anxious days Mary and Joseph searched for Jesus in the great city of Jerusalem. But they could not find Him anywhere.

Finally they went back to the temple, and there they found Him! He was sitting among the learned men who taught the law. He was asking them many questions, and listening seriously to their answers. Jesus was answering questions, too! The wise lawyers were astonished at the wisdom of the Boy. "And all that heard Him were astonished at his understanding and answers." This Boy was not an ordinary boy; every one

Mary and Joseph Searching for Jesus in the Great City of Jerusalem

of the chief priests and lawyers He met in the temple could tell that.

"Son, why hast thou thus dealt with us?" his mother asked Him. "Behold we have sought thee sorrowing." And Jesus answered, "How is it that ye sought me? Know ye not that I must be about my Father's business?"

Joseph and Mary did not understand just what Jesus meant, but Mary "kept all these sayings in her heart."

Jesus may have wished that He could remain in the temple with the learned men. But He was only twelve years old, just a boy, and the Hebrew law, which He loved, told Him He must obey those in charge over Him. And so He left the great temple in Jerusalem, and went back to Nazareth with Joseph and Mary.

Comprehension Exercise

Complete the sentences using the words below.

Passover
inn
Egypt
Nazareth

1. The Hebrew word "khan" means

   _____.

2. Joseph and Mary were told by an angel to take the baby Jesus into

   _____.

3. After Joseph, Mary, and Jesus returned from Egypt, they lived in

   _____.

4. When Jesus was twelve years old, He went with his parents to Jerusalem to celebrate the

   _____ Feast.

25 The King's Herald

Jesus had a cousin named John who was just a few months older than Himself.

John must have been a strange lad. He liked to live in the wilderness better than in big towns or cities. In a lonely place near the shore of the Dead Sea, John grew to be a man.

No people lived in this lonely place. There were not even many animals. Everywhere were bare rocks. A little grass and a few bushes and trees grew along the streams which emptied into the Dead Sea. The green waters of this sea were much too salty to be good for plants or trees to drink.

John could not live in this wilderness as he would have lived in a town or city. He wore unusual clothes—only a coarse camel's hair shirt, and a rough hair cloak. His long hair fell over his shoulders. He carried a long staff. When he was hungry, he would thrust the staff into holes between the rocks. Then he would dig out the honey which bees had stored there. He lived on this honey, and on grasshopper-like insects called locusts. The people in his country ate them and thought them a very good food.

John liked to be alone so that he could think about God. He was getting ready to give the people a great message. For years they had expected God to send them a king.

John's work was to tell them that this King was already among them. John was his herald, sent beforehand by God to prepare the hearts of the people to receive their King.

John was not afraid to tell the people that they were wicked and must turn away from sin. Sometimes, he

John the Baptist Leaving the City to Wander in the Wilderness

would go into the cities to preach to the people, but always he would hurry back to the wilderness. John was watching all the time for the King who was to come to save Israel. As soon as he had pointed Him out to the people, his work would be over. John did not know yet that his own cousin, Jesus, was this promised King and Savior.

John became a very popular preacher. People did not wait for him to come into the cities to preach to them. They went out into the wilderness where John lived, and listened to him there.

Imagine a large lake with a winding, yellow river–the Jordan–flowing into it. Crowds of people are hurrying down to that lake. The strong rays of the sun have burned up nearly everything bordering the bank of the yellow river. The ground looks as though it had been baked. Bare, bleak hills stand guard like stern, grim-faced soldiers at each side of the yellow river. Down these hills comes a long procession of unhappy people.

There goes a Pharisee, wrapping his cloak more closely about him. Pharisees were very careful to keep all the rules and ceremonies of the written Jewish law, and so they thought they were better than other people. This

A Hebrew Tax Gatherer and a Roman Soldier on Their Way to the Wilderness

man is afraid that he will touch someone who, he believes, is not quite so good as himself. Here a sick-looking beggar goes stumbling slowly along. He is rudely shoved to one side by a sneering Sadducee. This was the name of a group of Hebrews who thought differently from the Pharisees. They, too, had a very good opinion of themselves and were filled with sinful pride.

Scribes, or lawyers, in their silken robes carefully pick their way through the crowd. A spot on their white gowns seems terrible to them, although they carry hearts of stone in their breasts. Over there are some soldiers with shining spears and glittering helmets. Here greedy tax gatherers hold their purses with long, lean fingers as they make their way across the sun-baked plain. Rich men on camels and old men with staffs in their hands are hurrying toward the shores of the Jordan. From Jerusalem they come, and from all over Judea. All of them are anxious to hear the words of this wild-looking man of the wilderness.

Standing on the bank of the river is the man they are coming to see. They no longer call him just John; they call him John the Baptist. This is because he baptizes people, or uses water, to show that a person is sorry he has been wicked and that he is going to serve God.

Everyone seems interested in John the Baptist's talk. Today he is telling them about trees, and he says that an unfruitful tree is useless and ought to be cut down and burned. John says that all wicked people, like unfruitful trees, are useless and worse than useless. Scribes and Pharisees scowl at this. Perhaps they are wondering if John means them, because they do so little good to others.

John urges the people to be baptized, to show that they are sorry for their sins. "Wash all the wickedness out of your hearts. Show by being baptized that you intend to stop sinning," John says. "Be kind. If you have two coats, give one of them to someone who has none. If you have plenty of food, give some to those who have little."

Then he speaks to the tax collectors. "Stop wanting to cheat people when you collect taxes, and take from them only what they owe." To the soldiers he says, "Be kinder, tell the truth about others, and don't grumble about your wages."

But John doesn't pay much attention to the proud Pharisees and the scoffing Sadducees. He calls them wicked because they pretend to be good and holy, while John knows that many of them are not half as good as some of the poor people they have treated cruelly.

Every time that John preached to the people, he told them that someone would come who would be much greater and mean much more to them than he did. John did not know just when this promised King of the Hebrew people would come, or how. But one day, while he was preaching there by the riverside, the One for whom they were all waiting came. He did not look at all like the sort of king the people expected, so no one but John knew Him. The people saw only a stranger from Nazareth, a young man who was supposed to be the son of Joseph, a carpenter. This man a king and the promised leader of the Hebrew people? Why, kings had rich purple robes and golden crowns!

This man was not even rich, for he walked, instead of riding. To the people, this kindly man from Galilee, with the simple clothing, looked just like one of themselves.

Jesus, the Nazarene, had come to be baptized by John. And John, the herald of the King, knew that this simple Galilean was really the expected King. "Behold the Lamb of God!" John told the people, pointing to Jesus as He walked by the riverside. Then, because Jesus asked him, John baptized Him. And John saw the "Spirit of God descending like a dove, and lighting upon Him."

John's great work was done. He had given the message which prepared the way for Christ. The "Lamb of God" was the promised Messiah, who was sent to save God's people from their sins.

Hurrying to Hear John Preach

Comprehension Exercise

Complete the sentences using the words below.

Messiah
Dead
sins
pride

1. John grew up near the

   _____ Sea.

2. When John preached, he told the people to turn away from their

   _____.

3. Pharisees and Sadducees were filled with sinful

   _____.

4. Jesus was the "Lamb of God" and the promised

   _____.

26 The Wedding Feast

JOHN 2:1—3:2

In the country of Palestine, where Jesus lived, weddings took place at night. There was always a noisy procession to the bride's house, with music, singing, and shouting. First came the musicians. Then followed the torch bearers, who made the way bright with their lights held high.

The guests in the procession carried lights, too. Last of all came the bridegroom and his friends. He would take the bride and her friends back to his house for a splendid feast. At the time of a wedding lighted lanterns were always strung across the street before the bridegroom's house. These lanterns would make everything look beautiful and bright.

It was to a wedding like this that Jesus and his mother were invited. It was in Cana of Galilee, not far from Nazareth, where Jesus lived.

Perhaps the bride and the bridegroom did not know that they had invited a very great Guest that evening. Jesus sat among the merry crowd with his mother and his disciples, those few friends who knew that Jesus was the promised King. These disciples followed Him wherever He went, to be near Him and to listen to Him and see His kind and wonderful deeds. Jesus always had the desire to do the work that His Heavenly Father gave Him. No matter what anyone's trouble might be, Jesus would always do something to honor His Heavenly Father.

In the midst of the merrymaking at this wedding at Cana, something went very wrong. At such a feast in Palestine, the bridegroom always offered his guests wine. It was a disgrace for the wine to run out before the guests had enough.

Mary, Jesus' mother, was watching the one who was managing the feast. "They have no more wine," she whispered to Jesus. She knew that the bridegroom was the one to supply the wine. Why did she tell Jesus, who was only a guest? Would He help them out of their trouble? His mother thought that He would, and she said to the servants, "Whatsoever He saith unto you, do it."

Near Him were some empty water jars. "Fill the waterpots with water," Jesus commanded the servants. When they had obeyed Him, He said, "Draw out now, and bear unto the governor of the feast."

The steward, or "governor of the feast," must have been much pleased as he tasted the delicious wine which the servants brought to him. He wondered why the bridegroom kept his best wine until the end of the feast. Neither the steward nor the bridegroom knew how the wine came to be in those jars. But the servants who put water into the jars and drew out wine–they knew.

Six jars of this rich wine were now waiting for the guests. Only a moment before, the jars had held nothing but water. Now they were brimming with wine. The Guest from Galilee had done this wonderful thing! It was the first miracle that Jesus did before the people.

27 At the Pool of Bethesda

JOHN 5:1—24

Near the sheep market in Jerusalem there was a large pool of water which the Hebrews called Bethesda. Around the pool were five big porches, and on these porches many people were sitting and lying. Most of them were very wretched, poor, or ill.

These people had come here for a very special reason. For Bethesda was no ordinary pool. The water in it was supposed to do wonderful things. Sometimes it was quiet and peaceful, and at other times it was unsettled and "troubled." And whenever the water changed and became "troubled," the people thought that an angel had ruffled it, and that it would cure the first person who stepped into it. No wonder that when the surface of the water was unsettled, all the people rushed into it! But think of the poor helpless ones who were not able to get into the pool by themselves. Who would help them?

Across the porch came One whose eyes were always looking for those people whom everyone else forgot. He stopped beside one of the sick people who were gathered near the pool. Jesus asked this poor fellow who had been ill a long, long time, if he wished to be made well.

"Sir," the man answered, "I cannot get into the pool quickly by myself, and I have no one to help me. So while I am trying to get to the pool somebody always gets into the water ahead of me."

That poor helpless man! With shrunken arms and twisted legs, and his weak body, he was too feeble to

Jesus Healing the Sick Man at Bethesda

do anything but lie on his rug bed of wool or sheepskin, near the pool. Every time the water changed, he hoped that someone would be kind enough to help him into the pool.

How amazed he must have been to hear the voice of Jesus saying to him, "Rise, take up thy bed, and walk." Imagine his astonishment as strength came into his weak body. His twisted legs were well again, and the man stepped firmly upon the ground. There he stood–cured. But before he had time to get over his amazement and thank the One who had healed him, Jesus had passed on, out of sight.

Passing back and forth along the porches were chief priests, Pharisees, teachers of the law, and busy merchants. Rich and poor, young and old, passed the pool. Yet among them was only One who came to help; only One who was able to say to the sick man, "Rise and walk."

Comprehension Exercise

Complete the sentences using the words below.

Mary
wine
Bethesda
walk

1. Jesus turned water into

   _____ at a wedding in Cana.

2. Sick people often visited the pool called

   _____.

3. Jesus told the sick man to "Rise and

   _____."

4. _____ told Jesus that there was no more wine at the wedding feast.

28 Through the Roof

MARK 2:1—12

Jesus had gone to a town in Galilee named Capernaum. He was preaching to a crowd of people who had gathered in the little house where He was staying. For miles around people had come to see and hear Him. They were packed so closely together around the doorway that no late comer could get in.

Along the street came four men. They walked slowly and carefully, for they were carrying a bed on which lay a man who had the palsy. He could do nothing for himself; he could move only with the help of other people. The four men who were carrying him made their way through the crowd until at last they reached the door. But they could not get into the house, because of the people crowded around the door.

Did the four men turn away, planning to come back some other time? No, they did a surprising thing. This house, where Jesus was preaching, was only one story high. There were outside steps leading to the flat roof. Up those steps went the four men, carrying the bed. There on the roof they put down the bed very carefully. Then they began to tear up the roof. Those little houses in Palestine were often built with tile roofs which could easily be taken apart.

This house must have had such a roof, for the four men soon were able to make a large opening in it. Then down through the opening the men lowered the bed with their helpless friend on it. Right in the midst of the crowd, just at the feet of Jesus, the bed rested. Above, on the roof,

Lowering the Sick Man through the Roof

peering through the opening they had made, were those four friends. How anxiously they must have watched to see what would happen in the room below! These men were sure that Jesus would cure their sick friend.

Jesus was pleased with their faith in Him and He rewarded it. "Son, thy sins be forgiven thee," He said to the helpless man.

Now the scribes and Pharisees who were watching thought in their hearts, "Why does this Man speak thus? Who can forgive sins but God?" Jesus knew what they were thinking. So He said to them, "Why reason ye these things in your hearts? Whether is it easier to say to the sick of the palsy, 'Thy sins be forgiven thee'; or to say, 'Arise, and take up thy bed, and walk'?"

Then Jesus told the unbelieving scribes and Pharisees that He had power both to forgive sins and to heal sickness. So, turning to the helpless man on the bed before Him, He said, "Arise, and take up thy bed, and go thy way into thine house."

At these words the sick man was cured, and he stood up. He picked up his bed of rugs and blankets. Then he walked toward the door.

The Man Takes up His Bed and Walks

No doubt his four friends hurried down from the roof to greet him. What a happy meeting that must have been! As the five men walked away together, they must have talked of nothing but the great and healing power of Jesus.

29 Feeding Five Thousand People

MATTHEW 14:13—21

Everywhere Jesus went, eager people pushed and shoved one another aside as they tried to reach Him. They needed his help, and He healed people as often as it pleased His Heavenly Father. Even when Jesus wanted to rest, or to talk alone with his disciples, the people crowded around Him.

One time Jesus' twelve disciples were very tired. At last Jesus said to them, "Come ye yourselves apart into a desert place, and rest a while."

They climbed into a boat, and rowed across the lake. But the people would not be left behind. They hurried around the lake to the lonely hillside where the boat was heading. Probably others joined them on the way. And so fast did the people walk, that when Jesus and his disciples came to the other shore they found the people there, waiting for them.

How disappointed the tired disciples must have been! Here were the people again, asking for help. And they themselves were so tired! But Jesus felt sorry for the people, "because they were as sheep not having a shepherd: and He began to teach them many things." And He healed those among them who needed healing—the lame, the blind, and the crippled.

When it grew late in the day, and the people were still there, the disciples became worried. They went to Jesus and said, "Send them away, that they may go into the country round about, and into the villages, and buy themselves bread: for they have nothing to eat." Much to the disci-

**Jesus and His Disciples
Reach the Shore**

ples' surprise, Jesus answered them, "Give ye them to eat."

"Shall we go to the nearest town and buy food?" the disciples asked. "How many loaves have ye?" Jesus asked them. "Go and see."

When the disciples looked, they found there were five loaves of bread and two fishes. Jesus commanded that they be brought to Him. The disciples obeyed, probably wondering how Jesus was going to feed five thousand people with five round loaves and two small fishes.

First Jesus commanded the people to sit down on the grassy hillside. He had them sit in groups, with fifty or a hundred people in each group. Then He took the five loaves and the two fishes and, looking up toward heaven, He blessed them and gave thanks.

The watching people and the disciples too, perhaps, were thinking, "How can so little food feed so many?" But as they watched Jesus break the bread and the fish into pieces, they saw the piles of food grow bigger and bigger.

Now the disciples took great baskets of bread and fish, and gave to the people all they could eat. And after the people had eaten all they

Jesus Praying on the Mountainside

wanted, there were still twelve baskets full of bread and fish left over!

Then Jesus asked the disciples to go back across the lake in the boat without Him. He was going to send the people home. After that, He wanted to be alone in prayer with his heavenly Father.

Comprehension Exercise

Complete the sentences using the words below.

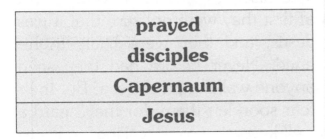

prayed
disciples
Capernaum
Jesus

1. Jesus healed the man with the palsy in the town of

   _____.

2. _____ was pleased with the faith of the four men who were trying to help their sick friend.

3. The _____ found five loaves of bread and two fishes.

4. Jesus fed over five thousand people and then

   _____ to His Heavenly Father.

30 On the Sea of Galilee

MATTHEW 14:22—36

Jesus' disciples had started across the Sea of Galilee as Jesus had told them to do. The five thousand people had all been fed from the five loaves and two fishes, and Jesus had sent them home, and had gone to a near-by mountain to pray.

Now the disciples were having a hard time with their little boat, for the water was rough. Although they rowed with all their strength, their boat did not seem to move through those rough waters. The wind blew them back, and they could not pull against it.

On the mountain Jesus must have known that his disciples were in trouble. Quickly He went down to the lake. There He could see his disciples, tossed about in their little boat on the rough sea.

The wild winds and fierce waves did not bother the Master. He saw that his disciples needed Him, and He went to help them. Right out on the stormy sea Jesus walked. Straight toward the tossing boat He walked upon the sea.

The disciples saw Him coming, but at first they were not sure that it was Jesus, and they were badly frightened. Never before had they seen anyone walking on the sea. But their fear soon left them, for they heard a well-known voice calling out to them, "It is I; be not afraid."

Peter wanted to be very sure his eyes did not deceive him. "Lord," he said to Jesus, "if it be Thou, bid me come unto Thee on the water." And Jesus answered, "Come."

Out of the boat Peter scrambled, and stepped bravely upon the sea. He walked toward Jesus. But all at once he took his eyes off Jesus and noticed the wildness of the storm. Then he was afraid, and he began to sink. "Lord, save me," he called to Jesus.

The Master stretched out his hand to Peter and caught him. Jesus must have looked sad when He said to Peter, "O thou of little faith, wherefore didst thou doubt."

Then Jesus and Peter stepped into the boat. The wind died down, the stormy waves grew quiet and the little boat brought Jesus and the amazed disciples safely to land. The disciples were amazed at the power of Jesus and said, "What manner of man is this that even the winds and sea obey Him?"

Shortly before Jesus returned to His Heavenly Father, He told His disciples just how powerful He was. Jesus said, "All power is given unto Me in Heaven and on earth."

31 The Good Shepherd

MATTHEW 18:11—14 AND JOHN 10:1—18

In Palestine, at the time of Jesus, there were many, many sheep. The shepherds who cared for them often knew every sheep in their flocks. Sometimes they could call each one by its name.

Imagine an early morning at a sheepfold in Palestine in those days:

The door of the sheepfold opens, and out comes the shepherd. His rough sheepskin mantle is thrown over his shoulders and he carries a long crook or staff.

One by one the sheep come through the gate and follow the shepherd. He knows where there is a fine pasture filled with green grass. A sparkling stream of cool water ripples across the green field. It is a long way to that pasture. The sheep will have to travel through a lonesome, rocky valley before they reach it. But the shepherd goes before them.

The pasture is reached at last. How the lambs frolic about! All day long the sheep and lambs stay in this beautiful pasture.

At last the shepherd looks at the sky. It is late afternoon, and a storm is coming. The sheep are a long way from home and the sheepfold. He calls to them, and they know his voice. Off they move homeward.

The gatekeeper is watching for them. He opens the door of the sheepfold when he sees them coming. The shepherd stands by the open door with his shepherd's staff raised. One by one, the sheep and lambs pass under his staff and through the gate into the fold. Hear

**The Shepherd Leading His Sheep
to the Green Pasture**

the shepherd counting the sheep as they pass in, "Ninety-seven, ninety-eight, ninety-nine-" Then he drops his staff and exclaims, "Only ninety-nine! One must be lost. I had a hundred sheep this morning."

Off he goes in the darkness and storm, calling the one missing sheep by name as he feels his way along the rough valley. He stops. A faint, sound reaches his ear. The lost sheep must have taken shelter in some cave among the rocks. The shepherd follows the sound of its voice. He finds the sheep, picks it up, and starts for the sheepfold.

As soon as the shepherd reaches the fold in safety, he calls his friends together.

"I have found my sheep!" he tells them. "Rejoice with me; for I have found my sheep which was lost." And his friends are glad, and rejoice with him.

How happy the listening people must have been when Jesus told them that God was like a good shepherd hunting for his lost sheep, and that God rejoiced more over wicked people who became good than over all the people who thought themselves perfect.

Bringing Home the Lost Sheep

Jesus knew that a good shepherd loved each one of his flock. "I am the Good Shepherd, and know my sheep, and am known of mine," He told the people. And He told them that like a good shepherd He, too, was ready to lay down his life for his sheep.

Comprehension Exercise

Complete the sentences using the words below.

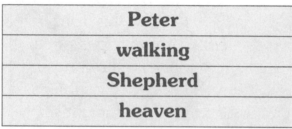

| Peter |
| walking |
| Shepherd |
| heaven |

1. Jesus came to His disciples

   _____ on the water.

2. _____ took his eyes off of Jesus and began to sink.

3. God knows where all His lost sheep are hiding and He will bring them to

   _____.

4. Jesus said, "I am the Good

   _____."

32 The Good Samaritan

LUKE 10:25—37

People were always asking Jesus questions. Sometimes they truly wanted to know the answer, but sometimes they were only trying to see what Jesus would say.

Once, when Jesus was talking to the people, a lawyer stood up and asked Him, "Who is my neighbor?" The lawyer had been repeating that part of the law which said, "Thou shalt love thy neighbor as thyself."

Instead of answering him with a few words, Jesus told him this story;

A Hebrew was traveling all alone from Jerusalem to Jericho. In a very lonely spot this Hebrew was attacked by thieves. His clothes were torn from him and his money was stolen. Then the cruel thieves beat the poor man and left him lying by the roadside.

The wounded Hebrew lay where he had been left, half dead. No one was anywhere near to help him.

At last a Hebrew priest came slowly along. He was on the opposite side of the road from the wounded man. He looked across toward the helpless man, but he did not cross over to his side. He drew his robe more closely about him, and passed by on his way to Jericho. He did not think he was cruel. He only thought, "That man is not one of my neighbors. He is a stranger to me. Why should I stop to help him?"

Later on a Levite, or Hebrew teacher, came hurrying along the road. He paused when he reached the wounded man. He looked closely at him, then turned away without offering any help. The man lying in

The Good Samaritan on the Jericho Road

the road was not one of his neighbors. Perhaps the Levite thought, "I should be foolish to stay in this dangerous spot just to help a stranger."

Then along the lonely road came a donkey and his rider. A man from the country of Samaria was riding on the back of his little animal. The Samaritan saw the wounded man. He stopped his donkey, jumped off, and ran to the man's side. The Samaritan saw that the man lying at his feet was a Hebrew. The Samaritans and the Hebrews hated each other, and did not call each other neighbor. But this Samaritan felt sorry for the poor man. He would not let this man die on the roadside.

"This man needs my help," the Samaritan thought. So he bound up the stranger's wounds, pouring healing oil on them. Then he helped the Hebrew to his feet and lifted him onto the back of his own donkey. The good Samaritan walked beside the poor man until they reached an inn. All night he stayed with the man and cared for him.

In the morning the Samaritan had to leave. But he knew that the Hebrew was not yet well enough to travel. So when the Samaritan left, he gave the landlord some money, and asked him to take care of the Hebrew until he was able to go home. "And if this is not enough," the Samaritan told the landlord, "spend more, and when I come again, I will repay you."

Jesus turned to the young lawyer. "Which now of these three," He asked him, "thinkest thou, was neighbor unto him that fell among the thieves?" The lawyer answered, "He that showed mercy on him." And as he turned to go, Jesus said to him, "Go, and do thou likewise."

33 The Prodigal Son

LUKE 15:11—32

Jesus told a story to the Pharisees and scribes who found fault with Him for talking so much with people who had done wrong:

There were once two brothers. These two brothers had everything they needed to make them happy. When they grew to be men, the younger one wanted to leave home. He asked his father to give him his share of the family wealth, and to let him go to visit other countries.

So this young man took all that belonged to him, and traveled far from home. He made new friends, but they were not true friends. It was easy for them to coax his money away from him, and to tempt him to do wrong things. For this younger brother was not wise. But when his money was gone, and he could not buy any more rich gifts for his companions, they deserted him. Soon he did not have money enough even to buy food for himself. A farmer from this country who kept many pigs needed a man to take care of them, and the young man was glad to be able to find this work. He knew that this would keep him from starving, because he could eat some of the food that was given him for the pigs.

But how cold and ragged and dirty he was! He had no friends, and only pigs for companions. He threw himself upon the ground and cried bitterly as he thought of his father and his beautiful home far away. Even his father's servants were better off than he was now.

Suddenly he jumped up. "I will arise and go to my father," he said to himself. "I will tell my father of my wickedness. I will tell him that I am no

The Prodigal Son Making Merry with His Foolish Companions

more worthy to be called his son. 'Make me as one of thy hired servants,' I will say to him."

So the young man returned to his father's home. "But when he was yet a great way off, his father saw him, and had compassion, and ran, and fell on his neck, and kissed him." Then the son told the father of his wickedness, just as he had promised himself he would do.

His father forgave him gladly, and to show his forgiveness he gave him a beautiful robe, and shoes, and a ring. And he ordered a great feast to be made for the son who had returned to him.

When the elder son came in from the field where he had been working, he heard the music and dancing at the feast. And when he learned that the feast was given because his younger brother had returned, the elder son was angry, and would not go into the house. So his father went out to talk with him. But the elder son would not listen. "I have stayed at home and worked and done right," he said to his father, "but you never gave me a party for my friends. Now as soon as this foolish young brother of mine comes home, you have a great feast for him."

The Elder Son is Angry

The father answered, "Son, thou art ever with me, and all that I have is thine. It was meet that we should make merry, and be glad: for this thy brother was dead, and is alive again; and was lost, and is found."

Comprehension Exercise

Complete the sentences using the words below.

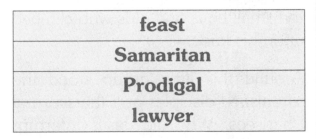

feast
Samaritan
Prodigal
lawyer

1. The good

   _____

   helped someone who was hurt
   even though he was a stranger.

2. Jesus taught the young

   _____ what
   it means to be a good neighbor.

3. The _____Son
   lost all of his money, friends, and
   food before he decided to ask for
   forgiveness.

4. The father was so glad that his
   son asked for forgiveness that he
   held a great

   _____.

34 Blessing the Children

MATTHEW 19:13—15

Many men and women came to Jesus and brought others for Him to help and bless. But these were not the only ones whom Jesus blessed. Little children were brought to Him too, so that He would put his hand on their heads.

One day the disciples were angry at the noisy chattering coming from a group of women and little children who drew near to Jesus.

"Don't you know the Master is too busy to be bothered with children?" some of the disciples said.

The poor, disappointed women turned to go away. A simple prayer from the Master as He laid his hands on the little heads was all the women asked. And the disciples refused them this!

But only for a moment were the mothers disappointed. They heard a voice telling them to stay. It was Jesus, calling to them to bring the little ones to Him.

Gently He took the babies in his arms. Softly He stroked the heads of the small boys and girls who climbed upon his knee.

Around this little group stood the astonished disciples and the scornful Pharisees. Why did Jesus interrupt his words with them, the Pharisees thought, just to please some foolish mothers and their little children.

Jesus knew what was in their minds. He held a little child out toward the people and said, "Suffer little children to come unto Me, and forbid them not: for of such is the kingdom of God."

SUFFER THE LITTLE  TO COME UNTO ME, AND FOR- THEM FOR OF SUCH IS THE -DOM OF GOD

MARK 10:14

35 Behold Your King!

LUKE 19:28—44

It was again the time for the Feast of the Passover. Many people were wondering whether Jesus would dare go to Jerusalem to celebrate this yearly feast.

They knew that the Pharisees and the Scribes, and the chief priests too, were Jesus' enemies, and that these people wanted to kill Him.

Jesus knew this too, but he did not hesitate about going to Jerusalem for the Passover. He told his disciples where they were to find a colt–a colt no one had ever ridden before. He told them to tell anyone who asked them why they were taking the colt, "The Lord hath need of him."

So the disciples brought the colt to Jesus. They put their cloaks over his back and set Jesus upon him. And so they started to go the few miles from Bethany, where Jesus was, to Jerusalem.

Down the road a little band of people waited for them. The eyes of all rested lovingly upon the One who was the center of the group. Jesus, as He rode along, was joined by throngs of people. Like Himself, they were on their way to Jerusalem for the Passover.

Among those who crowded about the Master were some who once had been lame or palsied. Others were there who had been blind, but now could see. Rich and poor traveled on camels and donkeys and afoot toward the city. Now and then a Roman soldier on horseback, with shield and spear glittering in the sunshine, rode past the long line of people. Little children ran in and out among the crowd. Perhaps some of them had been with the group of children whom Jesus had blessed. How happy they must have been to see the kind Master again!

Others were taking branches from the palm trees along the way, and tossing them on the road before Jesus. Many unfastened their outer cloaks and threw them upon the roadway for Jesus to ride over. "We do these things to honor kings," the people were thinking, "and so we do them for Jesus."

Jesus and his disciples could not get ahead very fast, for people from all

The Pharisees Plot Against Jesus

directions kept coming and crowding about Him. Many of them waved palm branches as they walked beside Jesus and his friends. "The Master is coming this way," the people shouted as they made their way toward Jerusalem.

Another crowd of people came out from the city to meet Jesus. They added their joyful cries to those of the people walking along with Him. "Hosanna!" they shouted again and again. "Blessed is He that cometh in the name of the Lord; Hosanna in the highest."

In that joyous throng were some who did not shout Jesus' praise. They were the Scribes and Phari-

sees. They, too, were on their way to Jerusalem to keep the Feast of the Passover. But they sneered at Jesus, and were annoyed by the people's praises of the Master. "What can we do to turn the people from Him?" they said to one another. "Behold, the world is gone after Him."

And some of them were so angered by the shouts of praise that they pushed rudely through the crowd until they reached Jesus' side. "Tell your disciples to stop their shouts of praise!" they told Jesus. But Jesus replied, "I tell you that, if these should hold their peace, the stones would immediately cry out."

The faces of the disciples walking close to Jesus grew serious and sad. They probably were thinking wonderingly of what He had told them a short time before. Behold, we go up to Jerusalem," Jesus had said; "and the Son of Man shall be delivered unto the chief priests, and unto the scribes; and they shall condemn Him to death, and shall deliver Him to the Gentiles: And they shall mock Him, and shall scourge Him, and shall spit upon Him, and shall kill Him: and the third day He shall rise again."

On the people moved, until they came within sight of Jerusalem. There Jesus stopped, and for a moment He looked at the beautiful city before Him. In the midst of it stood the temple, his Father's house. Jesus' eyes filled with tears. He could see ahead to the time when the temple and the whole beautiful city would be torn down and destroyed by its Roman enemies.

Again the crowd moved on toward Jerusalem. They marched through the great gates of the city. Among them rode the King, but none recognized Him as King except his disciples and a few other loving friends. "This is Jesus, the prophet of Nazareth of Galilee," the people of Jerusalem said. But the disciples shouted, "Behold your king!"

On the Steps of the Temple in Jerusalem

Comprehension Exercise

Complete the sentences using the words below.

Hosanna
children
colt
King

1. Jesus was happy to have the

   _____ come
   unto Him.

2. The disciples were told where they could find a

   _____ for
   Jesus to ride on.

3. The people shouted

   "_____" as
   Jesus rode up to the city of Jerusalem.

4. As Jesus entered Jerusalem, His disciples shouted

   "Behold your _____."

36 The House of Prayer

LUKE 19:45—48

The great temple in Jerusalem was surrounded by a number of paved courts or yards. In these courts one could hear lowing oxen, bleating sheep, and cooing doves. They were there, waiting to be sold. That was a strange place to-buy and sell, but these merchants did not think of the temple as a holy place. They did not care even if the birds and animals made so much noise- that the chief priests inside the temple found it hard to teach the people.

Besides the men who sold oxen, sheep, and doves, there were men around the courts, sitting at small tables. On these tables were piles of gold, silver, and copper coins. These men were changing into Jewish coins the money that strangers had brought with them into Palestine from their countries.

Into the courts of this beautiful temple came Jesus and his disciples. The Master had come to God's house to pray and to teach. The sick and the poor, the lame and the blind were following Him as they always did. From early in the morning until late at night they kept coming to Him for help.

The noise and shouting of the merchants buying and selling and making change must have made Jesus' face grow stern. The temple was no place for such things. But it did not matter, to the men buying and selling in the courts, that Jesus loved this sacred place. They did not care that He would use it only for healing and prayer. They were interested only in making money.

**Money Changers in
the Temple Court**

Jesus knew that the temple was his Father's house. It had been built for prayer, and as a shelter for all who were ill, poor, or unhappy. But many of these needy people had been crowded out to make room for cattle and money changers!

And so Jesus made a whip and drove all the merchants out of the temple. He overturned the money tables, and upset the seats of the sellers of doves. "It is written," Jesus said to them all, "My house is the 'house of prayer': but ye have made it a den of thieves."

After the traders had been cast out of the temple courts, Jesus and his disciples went into the temple. There they prayed, and there Jesus taught the people. "And the blind and the lame came to Him in the temple; and He healed them."

But while Jesus was teaching and healing people within the temple, the Pharisees and lawyers, and the chief priests within the temple were busy. They were planning to destroy the Master and to put an end both to Him and to his work.

Jesus Driving out the Merchants from the Temple Court

37 The Last Supper

LUKE 22:1—27

Jesus had told his twelve disciples just where they should eat the Passover Feast together with Him.

Because many Hebrew leaders in Jerusalem wished to kill Jesus, the disciples had not known where it would be safe for them to meet together for this solemn feast. But

**Jewish Family Prepares
for the Passover**

Jesus had known just where there was a man who had a guest chamber"–a large upper room furnished and prepared"–where He and his disciples could celebrate the Passover Feast together.

And when it was evening, Jesus and his twelve disciples sat and ate together in this room. The disciples were sad, because Jesus had told them that this would be the last supper they would ever eat together.

They were sure now that Jesus was going to be taken away from them. But sad as they were, the disciples began to dispute among themselves. They were quarreling over which one of them should be called the greatest. Each one was sure that he ought to be called the greatest. But Jesus said to them, "He that is greatest among you, let him be as the younger; and he that is chief, as he that doth serve."

Then Jesus rose from the table, put some water in a basin, and wrapped a towel about Himself. After that He washed the feet of his twelve disciples. In Palestine, washing a person's feet meant that one thought a great deal of that person and wished to serve him.

When Jesus came to Peter, Peter said to Him, "Thou shalt never wash my feet." But when Jesus answered,

"If I wash thee not, thou hast no part with Me," then Peter said, "Lord, not my feet only, but also my hands and my head."

Then Jesus said to them all, "I have given you an example, that ye should do as I have done to you." And he commanded them to "love one another." Now Jesus told his disciples something very surprising and very sad. "One of you shall betray Me," He said.

The disciples looked with amazement at one another. It did not seem possible that one of their own little circle would show Jesus' enemies where they could find Him.

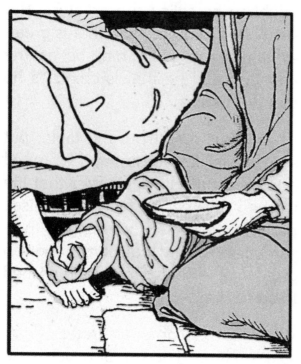

Jesus Washing Peter's Feet

And they said to Him one by one, "Is it I? And when Judas asked, "Master, is it I?" Jesus answered him, "Thou hast said."

But the others did not understand what Jesus meant when He said, "That thou doest, do quickly." They thought perhaps Jesus had told Judas of something he should buy for the feast, or of something he should do for the poor, because Judas was the disciple who kept the money for the little group. So the disciples did not question him when he left them and went out of the room.

Jesus talked very seriously with the other disciples. He told them not to be saddened by his death; He said that He would comfort them.

When Judas left the upper room where he had been eating the Passover Feast with Jesus and the other disciples, he went straight to the chief priests. They had promised to give him thirty pieces of silver if he would turn Jesus over to them. Judas agreed to sell Jesus into the hands of his enemies.

"Wait until night comes, then I will lead you to Gethsemane," Judas told the chief priests. "Jesus will be there alone with his disciples, and it will be easy for you to take Him."

"How shall we know Jesus in the darkness?" Jesus' enemies asked.

"Whomsoever I shall kiss, that same is He," Judas answered.

Comprehension Exercise

Complete the sentences using the words below.

Jesus
prayer
Judas
whip

1. Jesus made a

   _____ and drove the merchants out of the temple.

2. Jesus told the money changers that the temple was a house of

   _____, not a place for buying and selling.

3. The disciples were surprised when

   _____

   washed their feet.

4. _____

   helped the enemies of Christ for thirty pieces of silver.

38 In the Garden of Gethsemane

MATTHEW 26:36—57

High in the heavens, the moon shone down upon the beautiful Garden of Gethsemane, and cast its silvery light upon Jesus, kneeling in prayer. He had gone into a lonely part of the garden by Himself to pray. A little way off were the disciples, asleep under the olive trees.

Jesus had asked his disciples to watch with Him in this Garden of Gethsemane. They had walked there from the place where they had eaten their last supper together. All the way Jesus had talked to them, and told them what they should do after He left them.

Now as Jesus prayed to God for strength to go through the terrible experience He knew was ahead, the disciple's slept. "What, could ye not watch with Me one hour?" Jesus asked them when He came back to them. And again He went a little way off to pray. Once more the disciples fell asleep, and when Jesus came back to them they were ashamed, and did not know how to answer Him.

A third time Jesus went apart by Himself to pray. And for the third time the disciples fell asleep. But this time when Jesus returned, He said to them, "Sleep on now, and take your rest: behold, the hour is at hand, and the Son of Man is betrayed into the hands of sinners. Rise, let us be going: behold, he is at hand that doth betray Me."

At that very moment there was a noise at the entrance to the garden. Getting up, the disciples saw a crowd of men coming through the gate.

Seeking Jesus in Gethsemane

They were carrying lanterns, clubs, and swords. And with them walked Judas, the wicked disciple who had betrayed his Lord for thirty pieces of silver.

Judas gave the sign he had agreed upon with the chief priests. He walked up to Jesus and kissed Him.

Jesus did not try to escape from the men. He went up to them and asked them for whom they were looking. And when they said they were looking for Jesus of Nazareth, He answered, "I am He."

"And they laid their hands on Him, and took Him."

Then one of Jesus' disciples, Peter, drew his sword and cut off the ear of the high priest's servant. "Put up thy sword into the sheath," Jesus said to Peter. And He stretched out his hand and healed the servant's ear.

Jesus asked the men who had come out to take Him prisoner, why they had come to this lonely place armed with swords and clubs. "I was daily with you in the temple teaching," He said, "and ye took Me not." But they did not answer Him.

Then the men took Jesus away. Around Him were only people who hated Him. For his disciples, those friends who had promised to stay with Him, had left Him to his enemies, and had run away! And so they took Jesus to the home of the high priest, where the scribes and elders were waiting for Him.

39 Peter Denies Christ

MATTHEW 26:31—35, 69—75

One of Jesus' disciples, Peter, was a very hot-tempered, quick-speaking man. He loved Jesus, and at the last supper he was brokenhearted when Jesus told the disciples that He was going to leave them so soon. "Lord," Peter said, "I am ready to go with Thee, both into prison, and to death." But Jesus answered sadly, "I tell thee, Peter, the cock shall not crow this day, before that thou shalt thrice deny that thou knowest Me."

Peter could not believe that he could possibly tell people that he did not know Jesus-and three times! "If I should die with Thee," Peter told Jesus, "I will not deny Thee in any wise." And all the disciples said the same thing.

Yet after the men had come to the Garden of Gethsemane to take Jesus, every one of the disciples had run away. Even Peter was not brave enough to stay with his Master. But he did follow the mob as they took Jesus to the high priest's house, though he followed so far behind that no one could see him.

When they reached the high priest's house, Jesus was taken before the council of chief priests and elders. Peter went in and sat with the servants around a fire which they had built. And as he sat there, warming his hands, one of the maids looked at him closely and said, "You were with Jesus of Nazareth." But Peter denied this before all of them, saying, "Woman, I know Him not."

About an hour later someone else asked Peter if he were not one of Jesus' disciples. And Peter answered, "I am not." Then one of

"I do not know the man!"

the servants of the high priest, and a relative of the man whose ear Peter had cut off that very night, said to Peter, "Did not I see thee in the garden with Him?" Peter denied this, too.

But at that moment, as he was speaking, the long shrill crow of a cock rang out. Peter heard it, and remembered that Jesus had said to him, "The cock shall not crow this day, before that thou shalt thrice deny that thou knowest Me."

Peter rushed outside and there, where no one could see him, he cried very hard.

Poor Peter! He had been so badly frightened that he had forgotten Jesus' words. Perhaps, too, he had doubted the power of Jesus, because He did not strike back at his enemies. Peter forgot that Jesus had told his disciples that He must be crucified and buried, but that He would arise from the tomb and see and talk with them again.

Comprehension Exercise

Complete the sentences using the words below.

Gethsemane
Peter
cried
kissed

1. Jesus was taken by sinful men at the Garden of

   _____.

2. Judas walked up to Jesus and

   _____ Him as a sign to the wicked soldiers.

3. Jesus told _____ that he would deny Him three times before the cock crowed.

4. Peter _____ very hard after he had sinned against his friend, Jesus.

40 Calvary

MATTHEW 27:11—54

Along a narrow street in Jerusalem came a procession. It was not an orderly procession though, but a howling, shrieking mob. Some of the people in this mob were hurling stones and shouting ugly words at a prisoner who was being led out of the city. The prisoner was Jesus.

Jesus had broken no laws. He loved people and had been kind to them. He had healed them when they were ill. He had made blind eyes see, lame feet walk, and sorrowful men and women happy. In short, the Son of God, Jesus Christ, was a perfect and sinless man.

But many of the chief priests, scribes, and Pharisees wanted to kill Jesus. They were afraid of Him because of His words and His miracles. These wicked leaders did not want the people to love Jesus and call Him "King."

They could not understand a king who did not have a crown or a throne, and who ruled his people by love. "We will not have this man to rule over us," they said.

The high priest had taken Jesus to the Roman governor of the country to be judged. This governor, Pilate, had wanted to set Jesus free. "I find no fault in this Man," he had said. "I will let Him go."

But the angry crowd had cried again and again, "Crucify Him!" So at last Pilate had given Jesus to the crowd. And they had led Him away to crucify Him.

The soldiers placed a crown of thorns upon Jesus' head. His forehead was covered with scratches, and his back was bleeding from the lashes of stout whips. Across the

On the Way to Calvary

AND WHEN THEY HAD MADE A  OF

THEY PUT IT UPON HIS

AND A

IN HIS RIGHT

AND THEY BOWED THE BEFORE HIM, AND MOCKED HIM.

MATTHEW 27:29

Pharisees Mocking Jesus

shoulders of Jesus lay a cross. It was large, and much too heavy for Him to carry. Finally, the soldiers stopped a man who was passing, and made him carry the cross.

As Jesus went along, his enemies mocked Him by bowing before Him and sneering, "Hail, King of the Jews!" The scribes and Pharisees, the chief priests, and the angry crowd laughed at Jesus' suffering. The Man they hated was to be crucified, and they were so wicked that this made them glad.

The procession went to a little hill outside the walls of the city of Jerusalem. On this hill, called Calvary,

Jesus was nailed upon the cross, and left to hang there until He died.

On the cross above Jesus' head was placed the title, "Jesus of Nazareth, the King of the Jews."

For hours there was a strange darkness over everything. The clouds grew blacker and blacker, until at last it was as dark as night. Then, at the moment when Jesus died, there was a great earthquake; the earth shook, and rocks were split apart. In the temple the great veil, which set apart the holiest place in God's house, was torn in two from top to bottom. And the Roman soldier who guarded the cross where Christ hung cried out, "Truly this Man was the Son of God!"

41 Keeping the Promise

MATTHEW 28:1—8

The third morning after the crucifixion a few women who had sorrowed at Jesus' death came up the stony path toward the tomb where He had been laid. They had brought sweet spices to anoint his dead body.

"But how can we move away the large stone which stands before the tomb?" one of the women asked. "We shall have to do that before we can leave our spices."

"And what about the guard of soldiers around it?" another woman asked. For the chief priests and Pharisees had put soldiers to guard the tomb, because they had heard Jesus say that, even if they killed Him, in three days He would rise again.

The women toiled on up the steep, stony path, all of them wondering how they could get past the guard of soldiers, and who would roll away the great stone from the entrance to the tomb. But when they reached the place, they stood still in amazement. For not a soldier was in sight, and the entrance to the tomb was open! The heavy stone had been rolled away from before it, and the strong seal which had fastened it to the opening of the tomb was broken.

The women stooped down and looked inside the tomb. At first they thought it was empty. But after a moment they saw there in the darkness someone whose face shone with a wonderful light. He spoke to the women, telling them not to be afraid. "Ye seek Jesus of Nazareth, which was crucified," he said. "He is risen; He is not here."

The women knew that Jesus had said that He was going to live again. His words were true; his promise had been kept!

"Tell his disciples," the stranger with the shining face commanded.

Down the steep hillside the happy women ran, trembling "with fear and great joy." On they hurried, until they reached Jerusalem and the place where the disciples were. "The tomb is empty! Jesus, is not dead, He has risen!" the women joyously exclaimed. But the disciples did not believe them.

That same day, out in the country, a long way from Jesus' tomb, two sor-

**"He is risen!" the women
tell the disciples**

rowful men were walking. They were on their way from Jerusalem to a village called Emmaus. And as they walked, they talked together about Jesus.

A short time later, a third Man, a stranger, joined them. He asked the two travelers what they were talking about, so that He might join in their conversation.

They told the Stranger–who was Jesus, although they did not know this–that they were speaking of Jesus of Nazareth, a great prophet, who had been crucified. "We trusted," they said, "that it had been He which should have redeemed Israel." Then they told Him about the women who had gone to Jesus' tomb in the morning and had found it empty.

At this, the Stranger talked to them about the Scriptures. He spoke of Christ, and of the promises that had been made about his everlasting life: And as He talked the two men's hearts grew lighter. Slowly that awful memory of Calvary disappeared, and in their minds the men saw the Master they loved walk forth from his open tomb.

When they reached Emmaus, the two men invited the Man who had joined them to stop there with them. "It is toward evening," they told Him, and the day is far spent." So Jesus stopped with them and ate with them. "And their eyes were opened, and they knew Him; and He vanished out of their sight."

Why was it that we did not recognize Him while He was talking to us?" the two men asked each other. And they hurried back to Jerusalem to tell the eleven disciples that Jesus was alive, and that they had seen Him. As they spoke, Jesus himself appeared in the room. "Peace be unto you," He said. But the disciples were afraid, and did not believe that it really was Jesus. Then Jesus showed them his hands and his feet, torn by the nails which had fastened Him to the cross. And He talked to them, as He had talked to the two travelers, telling them that it had been necessary for Him to suffer and to die and "to rise from the dead the third day." At last the disciples believed. And when they believed, they were no longer sad.

Then Jesus told them that they should become apostles, or messengers, sent out by Him to tell others the story of his life and death and resurrection. All that Jesus had taught them was living in their hearts. Every one of them now wanted to go out and tell others that Christ had overcome death and purchased eternal life for those who love Him.

Comprehension Exercise

Complete the sentences using the words below.

Pilate
crucify
risen
three

1. The Jewish leaders cried out against Jesus saying,

   "_____ Him!"

2. The Roman governor,

   _____,

   wanted to set Jesus free.

3. Jesus told the people that

   _____ days
   after His death, He would rise from the grave.

4. The women who went to visit the tomb of Jesus were told by an angel that He had

   _____.

42 Breakfast By the Sea

JOHN 21:1—17

Very early one morning, soon after Jesus' resurrection, seven of Jesus' apostles were fishing in the Sea of Galilee. All night they had been out in their boat fishing, but not a single fish had come near their net. They were tired and hungry and discouraged.

Much to their surprise, as they looked toward the shore they saw Someone there, looking toward them. "Who can it be?" they asked one another. Then the Man called to them, "Children, have ye any meat?" "No," the apostles answered.

"Cast the net on the right side of the ship," the Man on the shore said to the apostles, "and ye shall find." Quickly the men threw the net on the other side of the boat. Down into the sea it sank. Then the men started to draw the net in again. It was so full of fish that they could hardly lift it in! The apostles gazed wonderingly at one another.

"It is the Lord," whispered John to Peter. Eagerly the apostles pushed the boat toward shore, dragging after them the great net filled with fine fish. But Peter was so impatient to see the Master that he cast himself into the sea and swam to shore.

At last all were together on the shore. The net was drawn in, full of great fishes. A fire of burning coals was waiting for the fishermen, and some of the fish were put upon it. There was bread, too. How good that breakfast of bread and broiled fish must have tasted after the long night on the water! And how happy those apostles must have been as they sat around the fire on the beach, talking with Jesus! This was the third time He had come to them after He had risen from the dead.

He asked the apostles if they loved Him, and He said to them, "Feed my sheep." For Jesus was the Good Shepherd, and many people all over the world were his sheep. He wanted his apostles to teach people everywhere what He had taught them.

Many days later Jesus walked out with his apostles from Jerusalem to Bethany. There He stopped, and gathering the apostles about Him, "He lifted up his hands, and blessed them." And as He blessed them,

"He was parted from them, and carried up into heaven."

The apostles understood now why Jesus had taught them so many things. They knew now that Jesus had left them, and that they must begin to tell others the Gospel of Christ. "And they worshipped Him, and returned to Jerusalem with great joy: And were continually in the temple, praising and blessing God."

43 Many Tongues

ACTS 1:1—15 AND 2:1—21

Jesus had told the apostles to wait in Jerusalem until a promise of power from heaven came to them. The apostles and Jesus' other friends met together often in a house where they were safe from their enemies. These enemies, the apostles thought, might kill them because they had been Jesus' followers.

Perhaps the scowling scribes and tricky Pharisees mocked them. Perhaps these enemies of Jesus said to one another, "We have killed their Master; soon we shall hear no more of these friends of his."

For several days and nights the little group of apostles remained together and prayed earnestly for God's blessing.

At last, one day the apostles heard a sound "as of a rushing mighty wind." It filled the whole house where they were. Then upon the head of each apostle there rested a wonderful light, like a tongue of fire.

And suddenly the apostles were filled with power from God the Holy Spirit. They began to speak to one another and, to their astonishment, they found that they could speak not only in their own Hebrew language, but also in other languages or tongues.

Now there were many people living in Jerusalem who had been born and brought up in other countries. When they heard about this strange thing which had happened to Jesus' apostles, they were amazed. "These men from Galilee never have been to our schools. How can they speak so many different languages?" they asked.

Upon the Head of Each Apostle Rested a Light Like a Tongue of Fire

These strangers in Jerusalem were glad to hear the apostles talk to them in their own familiar languages. And they were glad to hear the story of Jesus as the apostles told it to them. Now when night came, instead of a few faithful apostles praying together, there were hundreds of people who listened to the story of Christ and his wonderful works.

The people who had killed Jesus must have been frightened when they heard the apostles talking in many tongues. For instead of only a few people in Palestine knowing about Jesus, the whole world was beginning to hear of Him. The rich rulers and Pharisees had thought that they had silenced the disciples by crucifying Jesus. But now the apostles were telling the story of Jesus in every language, and to people of many different countries!

For a time the apostles stayed in Jerusalem, but soon all of them were eager to tell the good news to people in other cities and countries. And so they went everywhere, carrying with them the glad tidings of Jesus. They told people everywhere of the wonderful things He had said and done. And they told them, too, how Jesus had suffered and died for all who would trust in Him, and how He had overcome death just as the Scriptures had promised.

Comprehension Exercise

Complete the sentences using the words below.

sheep
Gospel
Apostles
Holy Spirit

1. The apostles had the duty to tell others about the

   _____ of Christ.

2. Jesus told His apostles to "Feed my

   _____."

3. The apostles were filled with power from God the

   _____ _____.

4. The Holy Spirit gave the

   _____ the power to speak in many different languages or tongues.

44 Peter, the Preacher

ACTS 10—12

As the months went on, more and more people believed that Jesus really was the Christ whom God had promised to send into the world. Many thousands of people became Christians, as Christ's followers were called. They often met together to study Jesus' teachings and to praise God the Father, God the Son, and God the Holy Spirit.

But the scribes and Pharisees were determined to stop the growth of Christianity. They forced the followers of Christ out of their homes. They stoned them, and whipped them, and put them into prison. But the more cruelly the Christians were treated, the larger their numbers grew and the stronger their belief in Christ became.

"Nothing seems to frighten them," the chief priests, scribes, and Pharisees said. "Soon the whole world will be running after them and becoming Christians."

Even though they said this, the Hebrew leaders did not really believe it. They did not know how hard the apostles would work to carry the teachings of Christ to others. But they did know that these friends of Jesus spoke earnestly and well of the things they believed so strongly. And the Hebrew leaders could see that, in spite of all their persecutions, every day more people became Christians.

Peter, the quick-tempered, and rash fisherman who had once denied his Lord three times, was now one of the best of the preachers.

This Apostle performed many wonderful deeds in the name of the Lord.

Peter was living at Joppa, a large seaport on the coast of Palestine. One day he went up on the flat roof of the house where he was staying, to pray. There it was quiet, and he could be alone.

Now Peter was very hungry. And after he had been praying for a while a strange thing happened. He thought he saw the heavens open above him and a great vessel come slowly down to him. It looked something like a huge sheet gathered up at the four corners. This sheet was full of animals– "all manner of four-footed beasts of the earth, and wild beasts, and creeping things, and

Peter's Vision on the Housetop

fowls of the air." And he heard a voice say to him, "Rise, Peter; kill, and eat."

But Peter had been taught not to eat the meat of certain animals, for in the Jewish law they were considered unclean. So he answered the voice, saying that he would not eat anything that was "common or unclean." Then Peter heard the voice a second time, and the voice said, "What God hath cleansed, that call not thou common."

Three times this strange vessel, which seemed like a great sheet filled with animals, was let down before Peter, and then drawn up to heaven. Peter began to wonder what this vision meant. Slowly he went down from the roof.

Three men were at the gate, waiting for him. "Will you come home with us?" they asked Peter. "Cornelius, our master, has sent for you. He and all his household wish to learn the truths about Jesus which you teach."

Now Peter knew the meaning of that strange vision upon the housetop. The men who had come for him were Gentiles, and the Jews had been taught to think of them as heathen. But Peter knew now that the vision had been sent to show him that God loved every one of his children—Jews and Gentiles alike. "God hath showed me that I should not call any man common or unclean," thought Peter.

Peter kept Cornelius' messengers with him that night, and in the morning he went back with them to the town where Cornelius lived. There he preached to many people who were not Jews, and they believed his words.

The new Christian church was growing so large that the scribes and Pharisees, chief priests and rulers were getting more alarmed than ever. "If we do not stop this new religion," they said, "we shall lose all our power over the people. Perhaps King Herod Agrippa will help us put an end to it."

So, to please the Jews who hated the apostles, Herod Agrippa killed the apostle James. Then, "because he saw it pleased the Jews," he took Peter and put him into prison.

At night Peter slept "between two soldiers, bound with two chains." But one night as Peter lay asleep on the cold stone floor a strange light shone into the prison. An angel of the Lord awakened Peter, and struck the heavy chains from his hands and feet.

"Arise up quickly," the angel said. "Cast thy garment about thee, and follow me."

It seemed like a vision to Peter, but he obeyed. Past the first and second

Peter Sleeping Between Two Soldiers

guards he went with his shining guide. No one tried to stop them. Perhaps the light that guided Peter blinded the soldiers who guarded the prison. The heavy iron gate of the prison opened of its own accord to let Peter and his guide pass through.

When Peter turned to thank the angel who had led him out of the prison, he found himself alone. "Now I know that my visitor was a messenger of God, sent to save me from King Herod Agrippa," Peter thought.

He hurried through the streets of Jerusalem to a friend's house. "Tell all the disciples that God has brought me out of prison. Their prayers for me have been answered," Peter said to his friends. But he could not stay with them, for he knew that when morning came Herod Agrippa would send his soldiers after him. So Peter hurried to a place many miles from Jerusalem, where he was safe from the cruelty of the king.

After his wonderful escape from prison, Peter talked all the more about Jesus and his power. Peter had once kept still because he was afraid. Now the apostle who had denied that he knew Jesus, was preaching his name everywhere. The power of the Holy Spirit made Peter bold.

45 Paul, the Great Missionary

ACTS 9

Paul, one of the greatest apostles of Christ, had not been a disciple of Jesus when the Master was on earth. In fact, after Christ's death Paul was for a while one of the worst enemies of Jesus' followers. But on the way to the city of Damascus, where he was going to persecute Christians, Paul had a strange experience.

As he was traveling along, a light brighter than the noonday sun suddenly shone around him. The fierce light blinded him, and he fell to the ground. Then he heard a voice saying, "Why persecutest thou Me?" And Paul cried out, "Who art Thou, Lord?"

"I am Jesus whom thou persecutest," the voice replied.

Paul, astonished and trembling, asked what he should do. And the voice told him to go into Damascus, where he would be told what he should do.

Paul arose. He still could not see, and his companions had to lead him into Damascus.

Paul was altogether changed. The Lord showed him that he must teach people that Jesus' religion was not only for the Jews but for all people everywhere. It was to be Paul's mission to carry this good news or gospel into other countries.

None of the other apostles could do this work as well as Paul. Paul was filled with a great love for Jesus and his followers. And he was not afraid of anything except the Lord.

A few days after Paul reached Damascus, his sight was given back to him, and he was baptized. Paul then went to the temple to preach to the people that Jesus was the Christ, the Son of God. The people who heard him were amazed that Paul, the man who had persecuted the Christians so bitterly, was now preaching the word of Christ. A short time later, the unbelieving Jews began to try to kill Paul, because he had become a Christian.

The apostles at first could not believe that Paul was their friend. But at last they became sure that he was a true

**Enemies of the Christians
Plan to Kill Paul**

Christian, and they welcomed him as an apostle.

Nothing discouraged Paul. He traveled all over the country, preaching. Everywhere he went he left behind him little companies of people who believed in Jesus and practiced his teachings. The learned people especially listened to Paul eagerly, because he was a well educated man and a Roman citizen.

Paul traveled to other countries and established Christian churches in many cities. But when he returned to Jerusalem, the enemies of the Christian people there had him arrested and brought before the Jewish council. The council could not decide what to do with Paul. So he was sent to the governor of the province. The governor could find nothing against him, but to please Paul's enemies he kept him in prison.

When Paul at last was tried he spoke before the governor and Herod Agrippa, the king of Palestine, with such power that the king said, "This man doeth nothing worthy of death or of bonds." They would have set him free, but Paul asked to go to Italy to be tried before the emperor at Rome. Paul had the right to do this, because he was a Roman citizen. Perhaps, too, he wanted a chance to preach about Jesus to the Roman emperor.

Paul Telling the King about Jesus

So Paul and certain other prisoners were put aboard a ship to sail for Italy. It was a long and dangerous trip, and winter came on before the ship was halfway there.

"Do not go any farther," Paul advised the captain and the Roman soldier who was in charge of the prisoners. "This winter voyage is too dangerous."

But the captain would not listen to him. He wanted to get to a good harbor located far away to spend the winter. So he sailed the ship far away from the calm harbor. A great storm came up; huge waves, driven by fierce winds, towered high above the ship and lashed its sides. The little boat was nearly torn to pieces by the sea.

As the storm kept on, everyone lost hope of ever reaching shore—everyone but Paul. "Be of good cheer," Paul said to them all, "for there shall be no loss of any man's life among you, but of the ship." Then he told them that in the night an angel of God had told him that everyone in the ship should be saved.

After being tossed about on the rough sea for days, the ship came near land. Here it began to break to pieces as the waves beat against it. Then the soldiers wanted to kill the prisoners, for fear they would swim to land and escape. But the captain of the soldiers would not allow this to be done. He "commanded that they which could swim should cast themselves first into the sea, and get to land: And the rest, some on boards, and some on broken pieces of the ship. And so it came to pass, that they escaped all safe to land." The people of the island greeted them kindly, and built a fire for them.

After three months Paul and his companions started again for Italy. This time there were no storms, and Paul at last reached Rome. He lived there for two years. And he "received all that came in unto him, preaching the Kingdom of God, and teaching those things which concern the Lord Jesus Christ, with all confidence, no man forbidding him."

Paul's enemies had not closed his mouth as they had wanted to do. Instead they had helped him to carry his message to people of other countries. Storm and tempest and angry sea could not stop Paul's tongue. Until he became an old man, he sailed over many seas, carrying the gospel to far away lands. Through strange countries he traveled, healing the sick and preaching the good news that God is love and that his beloved Son, Jesus, is both Savior and Lord.

Jesus is King Over All the Earth

Comprehension Exercise

Complete the sentences using the words below.

love
preachers
Gentiles
Paul

1. Peter became one of the best

   _____ in the early Christian church.

2. The vision Peter saw taught him that God loves every one of his children, Jews and

   _____ alike.

3. _____ was changed from being a hater of Christ to a wonderful Christian in the city of Damascus.

4. Paul preached the good news that God is

   _____.